Social Anxiety:

Ultimate Guide to Overcoming Fear, Shyness, and Social Phobia to Achieve Success in All Social Situations

© **Copyright 2015 - All rights reserved.**

In no way is it legal to reproduce, duplicate, or transmit any part of this document in either electronic means or in printed format. Recording of this publication is strictly prohibited and any storage of this document is not allowed unless with written permission from the publisher. All rights reserved.

The information provided herein is stated to be truthful and consistent, in that any liability, in terms of inattention or otherwise, by any usage or abuse of any policies, processes, or directions contained within is the solitary and utter responsibility of the recipient reader. Under no circumstances will any legal responsibility or blame be held against the publisher for any reparation, damages, or monetary loss due to the information herein, either directly or indirectly.

Respective authors own all copyrights not held by the publisher.

Legal Notice:

This e-book is copyright protected. This is only for personal use. You cannot amend, distribute, sell, use, quote or paraphrase any part or the content within this e-book without the consent of the author or copyright owner. Legal action will be pursued if this is breached.

Disclaimer Notice:

Please note the information contained within this document is for educational and entertainment purposes only. Every attempt has been made to provide accurate, up to date and reliable complete information. No warranties of any kind are expressed or implied. Readers acknowledge that the author is not engaging in the rendering of legal, financial, medical or professional advice.

By reading this document, the reader agrees that under no circumstances are we responsible for any losses, direct or indirect, which are incurred as a result of the use of information contained within this document, including, but not limited to, —errors, omissions, or inaccuracies.

Table of Contents

Introduction **10**

Chapter 1 – Anxiety 101 .... **11**

What Is Anxiety? 15

Anxiety Disorders 16

Anxiety Disorder Symptoms 18

Anxiety Disorders' Effects On Your Body 19

How Anxiety Can Impact Your Social Life 21

How Anxiety Can Ruin Your Chances For Success 21

Is There A Cure For Anxiety Disorders? 21

Chapter 2 – What Is Social Anxiety? **23**

Chapter 3 - What Causes Social Anxiety? **26**

Behavioral 26

Thinking 26

Evolutionary 27

Biological 27

Traumatic or Bad Experiences 27

The Demands of Life 28

Stresses of the Present 28

How All of These Factors Work Together 28

Chapter 4 - What Aggravates Social Anxiety? **30**

Unhelpful Thoughts 30

Avoidance 30

Using 'Safety Behaviors' 31

Increased Self-Focus 32

Food And Drinks 32

Chapter 5 – Instant Hits For Quick Social Anxiety Relief 35

Nothing 36

Don't Breathe Too Much 37

It Too Shall Pass 38

Talk To Yourself 40

Familiarity Anxiety 42

Chapter 6 – Self Help Tactics For Managing Your Social Anxiety 44

Worrying For Anxiety Relief 44

Know If The Anxiety Trigger Is Solvable 47

Banishing Unhelpful Thoughts 49

    Patterns Of Unhelpful Thinking 50

    Predicting the Future 50

    Mind Reading 50

    Taking Things Personally 50

    Over Generalizing 51

    Focusing on the Negatives 51

Reducing Internal Focus In Social Situations 52

Minimizing Or Stopping The Use Of Avoidance And Safety Behaviors 53

Cultivating Relationships 58

Mindfulness 59

    Stay In The Moment 61

    Learn To Radically Accept Things As They Are ... 62

    Counter Talk 62

    Think About Your Breathing 63

    Scan Your Body 64

Chapter 7 – Professional Help: Therapy 65
Cognitive Behavior Therapy (CBT) 65
    Identify 66
    Evaluate 66
    Replace 67
Hypnotherapy 67
How Does Hypnotherapy Work? 68
What Happens During Hypnotherapy? 69
Does Hypnotherapy Really Work for Social Anxiety Disorder? ... 69

Chapter 8 – Professional Help: Prescription Medicines 71
Tranquilizers 72
Anti-Depressants 73
Buspirone 74
Beta Blockers 75
More Caution 75
Final Word On Prescription Medicines 76

Chapter 9 – Nutritional Tactics For Social Anxiety . 77
Whole Foods To Enjoy 77
Herbs 79
Supplements 81
Supplementary Caution 83
How to Create an Anti-Anxiety Diet 84
6 Foods That Help You to Fight Anxiety 86

Chapter 10 – Complementary and Alternative Treatment for Social Anxiety Disorder 88
Relaxation and Stress Techniques 88
    Diaphragmatic Breathing 89

How to Practice Diaphragmatic Breathing 89
Progressive Muscle Relaxation 90
How to Practice Progressive Muscle Relaxation 91
Autogenic Training 93
How to Practice Autogenic Training 94
Guided Imagery 95
How to Practice Guided Imagery 96
Meditation 97
History of Mindfulness Meditation 97
What is the Goal of Mindfulness Meditation? 98
How Does Mindfulness Meditation Work? 98
Yoga 101

Chapter 11 - Homeopathic Approach to Social Anxiety Disorder 106

Ambra Grisea 106
Argentum Nitricum 107
Baryta Carbonicum 107
Ignatia 108
Lycopodium 108
Aconite 108
Passionflower 109
Gelsemium 109
Evening Primrose Oil 110

Chapter 12 - Using Thought Records for Social Anxiety Disorders 111

Using Thought Records 112
Unhelpful Thoughts 112
How to use Thought Records 113

The activating event...113
The consequences of the event..113
Your beliefs about the event 114
Your unhelpful thought styles 114
Your one unhelpful thought...114
Replacing that thought..114

Chapter 13 – Let's Get Physical…And Calmer 116
Exercise And Physical Activities: One And The Same? 116
The Right Intensity For Anxiety Management 117

Chapter 14 – Social Anxiety In Children................. 119
Performance And Interaction...119
How Do Children Get It?..120
Does Your Child Have Social Anxiety Disorder? 120
Treatments 121
    Behavioral Therapy...122
Prescription Medicines...122

Chapter 15 - 11 Things You Should Do if You Have Social Anxiety Disorder 123
1. Start Socializing...123
2. Get Some Help..123
3. Develop Some Healthy Habits 123
4. Read 124
5. Keep a Journal...124
6. Congratulate Yourself...124
7. Write Your Goals Down..124
8. Become Your Own Advocate...125
9. Practice Your Social Skills...125
10. Practice Assertiveness Skills...125

11. Share Your Experiences 126

Chapter 16 - 10 Things You Need to Stop Doing if You Have Social Anxiety Disorder 127

1. Stop Avoiding 127
2. Stop the Negative Thoughts... 127
3. Don't Put Off Getting Help 127
4. Stop Believing That There is No Hope 128
5. Stop Comparing Yourself 128
6. Stop Telling Yourself You Can't Change 128
7. Stop Predicting That You Will Fail 129
8. Stop Missing Opportunities 129
9. Stop Keeping Your Disorder a Secret 129
10. Stop Believing That You Suffer Alone 130

Chapter 17 - 8 Things People with Social Anxiety Want 131

1. Connection 131
2. Understanding 131
3. Solitude 131
4. Stability 132
5. Peace 132
6. Confidence 132
7. Fulfillment 133
8. Growth 133

Chapter 18 - 10 Anxiety Myths Busted 134

Anxiety Disorders Are Not Real Illnesses 134
Panic Attacks Make You pass Out or Lose Control 135
People With Anxiety Should Avoid Stressful Situations 135

You Should Always Have a Paper Bag In Case Of
Hyperventilation 136

Some People are Habitual Worriers and Can't Be Treated 136

Anxiety Disorders are Uncommon 137

Anxiety Will Get Better On Its Own 137

I Just Need a Drink or a Smoke to Get Through It 138

Therapy Will Take Up the Rest of My Life 138

You Can Snap out of Anxiety 139

Chapter 19 - Frequently Asked Questions about Anxiety Disorders 140

What are the most common anxiety disorders? 140

What is generalized anxiety disorder? 140

What is obsessive compulsive disorder? 140

What is panic disorder? 141

What is post traumatic stress disorder? 141

What is social anxiety disorder? 142

What is stress? 142

What are the main symptoms of stress in adults? 142

Are there any coping strategies that can help? 143

Conclusion 144
Bonus 146
Recommended Reading 147

Introduction

"We are disturbed not by what happens to us, but by our thoughts about what happens"

Greek philosopher Epictetus

Of course, if you suffer from social anxiety, you could add to that quote by adding the words "or what might happen" to the end. Social anxiety is a highly debilitating condition, leaving sufferers as complete nervous wrecks, no matter what the situation.

There are always going to be people who tell you to "pull yourself together", without realizing exactly what it is you are going through, even though they themselves may feel of touch of anxiety when they are nervous or fearful about something. The fact is, social anxiety is a big issue, leading to far bigger symptoms and having a serious impact on life.

If you are suffering from social anxiety disorder, if you feel that others are judging you for being nervous, shy or fearful of a situation then you have come to the right place. In this eBook, I am going to show you how to overcome this, how to get back your confidence and how to regain the life you once had.

Chapter 1 – Anxiety 101

"If you don't think your anxiety, depression, sadness and stress impact your physical health, think again. All of these emotions trigger chemical reactions in your body, which can lead to inflammation and a weakened immune system. Learn how to cope, sweet friend. There will always be dark days." – Kris Carr

Before we go specifically into social anxiety, allow me to share with you my own experience with it as well as explain anxiety in general so you can better appreciate the things I'll be sharing with you concerning social anxiety. Here goes.

Almost every week, I go up on stage to address more than 1,000 people during our church service. Many times, the topic that I'm expected to talk about for a given weekend service is given to me at least 7 days prior. There are times, however, that I'm only given a day or 2 to get ready. Even more exciting than that, there were – and still are – an instance or two when I'm asked to substitute for the assigned person at the start of the service itself.

Would you believe me if I tell you – and I don't mean to brag – that it doesn't bother me anymore whether I'm given a week or minutes to prepare? Here's more – would you actually believe me if I told you that I used to be a nervous wreck even just talking to a girl that I like or having to make small talk to anyone? You may be wondering, how'd that happen? Well, here's my story.

I used to be really, really shy. Like I said, even the prospect of having to make small talk is enough to make me sweat blood. To me, engaging a totally random stranger for small but rational talk is just about as risky as approaching the same but yelling at his or her face "I am weird!" How weird is that, huh?

But that was a long time ago. Like I wrote earlier, I'm now at a point where I'm very comfortable standing in front of more than 1,000 people on any given Sunday almost every week. What happened, you may ask. Well, as much as my humble self would like to take all the credit for the 180-degree turn, sadly I can't. I would say it was really God's hand that led me to situations that molded my personality and allowed me to overcome my social anxiety.

My father's unexpected – and in my view, untimely – death in 2000 compelled me to seek answers as to why it happened and to look for a way to strengthen myself in moving on with life. It so happened that there was an upcoming orientation seminar for a group of single people in the church that I was going to at that time. Being quite the religious person that my parents raised me to be, I registered and attended that 13-week program.

At the end of that 13-week program came my first social anxiety baptism of fire: dance in public! I know for most people, it's a joy. But since I was a socially awkward and very shy person who happens to be as adept to dancing as Manny Pacquiao is to singing, for me it was a near-death experience!

Believe me, I tried exercising my right to vote myself out of it but all my other group mates outvoted me so against my will, I was forced to humiliate myself by dancing in front of people. Although we were in a group, I danced like a log so naturally, people's attention gravitated toward me – screaming my name. That made the nauseating and anxious sensation even worse. I wanted to both hide and puke. But I guess God (or whatever deity you believe in – or the cosmos) was real! I survived was able to go back to my normal, shy and away-from-people introverted life. Or so I thought.

For some strange reason, the powers that be in that church community thought I'd make for great leadership material. So after some pressure from leaders and an unforeseen covenant that I had to make with God, I decided to accept the position of heading the next batch's orientation program. This would mean that apart from overseeing other volunteers, I'll also be the speaker of last resort for each and every one of the 13 weekly talks, in case the designated speakers can't make it. What have I gotten myself into?

And exactly as I feared, a couple of the anointed speakers failed to make it to their talks so I had to anoint myself courageous and give those talks. No choice. Even if the audience was as many as 10 people only, to a socially anxious person that is equivalent to a filled-up Staples Center or Quicken Loans Arena. So after preparing my last will and testament, I gave those talks. And yet another funny thing happened.

I survived!

A couple of talks more with mostly friends as my audience, I slowly became more comfortable with speaking in front of people and in the process, I became more comfortable talking to just about anyone too. I was still shy and anxious, but it wasn't as bad as before. Probably it was because I felt that was as much public speaking I'll ever do in my life. Boy, was I wrong.

After several years in that community, I transferred to another church. Because the leadership in that church knew me personally, they were alright that I take a break from ministry and just be a member. But as with the previous one, I was eventually asked to speak in front of the general membership, although this time on an almost weekly basis and with a larger, less familiar crowd.

Here we go again...anxiety mode on!

One of the better things going on that time was the leadership let me take baby steps. From complete rest to giving me speaking assignments once a month until it became weekly. Then from the weekly introductions, they eventually upped the ante and let me preach on certain services. I became more and more confident and less anxious – again, not because of my efforts but because of the people who surrounded me and who pushed me – however gently – into the limelight.

But that wasn't the end of it yet. This was a group of people who, at most, numbered only 80. And because it was a small community church, they eventually became family and it came to a point that it was like the first time – mostly friends and family, albeit on a larger scale. And when I got married, I moved to my spouse's church – and that one was way bigger than mine.

Because it was a really big church (we're talking of at least 10,000 members attending 8 different weekend services), I felt at home being an ordinary member. Finally, I thought! I mean, with all the veterans and more eloquent speakers out there, I don't think I'll need to step up and speak on stage again. At least not on one where an average of 1,200 people attend every service.

Again, I was wrong.

Over the last 2 years, I found myself being led to different groups and leaders until I landed in the group of one of the senior pastors preaching in 3 of the 8 services. He lacked people to assist him, particularly with the transitions and exhortations prior to his preaching. Guess what? I was assigned again to speak in front – although this time, my anxiety level should've gone through the roof.

Me, talk in front of 1,200 people? I don't care how short my talks will be – that's 1,200 people! If I was so anxious with an average of 10 people, then 80, how much more I should've been if that average crowd was multiplied by 15!

Can you imagine my anxiety level by the time I stepped up on stage for my first ever gig in my current church? If I could sweat blood, I probably would've. I was palpitating and worse, my mouth and throat dried up even after downing a whole bottle of water minutes before. To my mind, all my preparations seemed to have been flushed away by my anxiety. But something was different.

This time, the anxiety wasn't as severe. In fact, I didn't tank my first 1,200-person talk on stage, unlike my first talk in front of 10 people. However, anxiety still affected me and I wasn't able to do as well as my previous talks in smaller venues. Understandable though – this was a crowd that's at least 15 times larger. But the rest was history. After almost 2 years of doing this already, I'm no longer anxious speaking in front of a crowd or making small talk with a complete stranger. It seems my social anxiety's gone for good. In fact, I'd say I don't panic or get anxious at the thought of speaking in front of more than 10,000 people anymore. It seems that 1,000 people was the tipping point at which I really overcame my social anxiety.

What Is Anxiety?

Simply put, it is a worried, nervous or uneasy feeling about an uncertain outcome. It's what you feel when you first asked your crush to your very first prom or if you're the girl, when your crush asked you out to your very first prom or date. It's the same feeling you get when you first biked without those training wheels or if you're the really daring type, when you first went skydiving. For those who are like me, it's the same feeling on your wedding day – at least your first one. Why? It's because these days, marriage is no longer the "certain" decision as it once was with the increasingly high rates of divorce all over the world.

Anxiety, however, isn't the same as disaster. Anxiety, at its simplest form, is just merely feeling worried or nervous. That's all there is to it. As such, pardon the pun but it shouldn't be something to worry about. It's human to be nervous and worry about things that normally would make most other people feel so too, such as speaking in front of 10,000 people or dancing in front of national television.

Anxiety disorders, however, are a different story altogether.

Anxiety Disorders

An anxiety disorder is an extreme form of your regular anxiety. It's actually considered a mental condition that can make you feel extremely distressed, scared or frightened in normal situations where just about everybody else feels comfortable, safe or secure. Under such situations, you can actually be rendered helpless, paralyzed or even immobilized by such feelings of fright to the extent that your daily, normal functioning is already impaired. Three of the most common anxiety disorders are:

- Generalized Anxiety: Intense, extreme and often out-of-this-world levels of nervousness and worry even under the most normal and safest situations.
- Panic: Feelings of terror that suddenly come out of nowhere often and regularly. Usually, a panic attack

manifests through chest pains, profuse sweating, a choking sensation or palpitations. The intensity of such usually leads to escalation as the person suffering from panic attacks may feel that either he or she's going nuts or is having a heart attack.

- Phobias: This refers to chronic extreme fear of particular objects or situations such as insects, flying in airplanes, dark rooms or riding a boat. What makes phobias rather excessive is when in avoiding the objects or situations being feared, your daily living is already hampered because you also avoid the daily important activities in your life.
- PTSD – Post-traumatic Stress Disorder usually develops when a person has seen or experienced something that is traumatic. Symptoms may begin straight away or they can come out weeks, months, even years later. Some of the most common causes include war, being physically assaulted, natural disasters, etc. and anxiety episodes can come on without any warning.
- OCD – Obsessive-compulsive Disorder is an anxiety disorder, although it is only just recently that it has been seen as such. People who have OCD usually find themselves having to repeat certain rituals over and over, including washing hands constant, counting, and checking something several times.
- Social Anxiety: A specific form of anxiety, this one's about interacting with people – social interactions and situations. This extreme sense of fear and worry about being with and around people is usually fuelled by worries of being ridiculed, rejected, embarrassed or simply being looked at in a negative light by other people. This is what we'll be talking about in all of the remaining chapters of this book.

Anxiety Disorder Symptoms

So how can you distinguish between regular anxiety and an anxiety disorder? Here are some regularly manifesting symptoms that may indicate you have an anxiety disorder:

- Sleepless Nights: Worrying makes sleeping as easy to do as sprinting for 1 kilometer on a steep uphill road or whispering to your friend in a rock concert. Why? It's because feeling this way elevates your heart rate, which heightens your senses at the time when you're supposed to be relaxing already.
- Sweaty And/Or Cold Feet And Hands: Because feeling anxious elevates your heart rate, your body draws more blood to areas that it believes need it more and in the process, reduce the amount of blood flowing to your extremities, particularly the hands and feet. As a result of less blood flow, the temperature in those areas tend to drop. Your body, however, may be fooled into thinking that the temperature in your hands and feet are the same as those body parts with increased blood flow and thus, signal them to sweat as if they're hot. Hence cold but sweaty hands and feet.
- Palpitations: One very obvious effect of anxiety is substantially elevated or stronger heart rate/beat. If this seems to happen often and without much reasonable basis, it's a potential sign of an anxiety disorder.
- Feeling Like You Can't Breathe: Anxiety – ordinary or disorders – make you breathe in more air than what's normal or required. When you do this – hyperventilate – your body's oxygen-carbon dioxide balance is severely disrupted, which makes you feel like you're not getting enough oxygen despite the overabundance of such.

- Can't Keep Still: All that adrenaline secreted by your body while it's in an anxious state makes you unable to stay still and makes you restless and on edge.
- Feeling Nauseous: When you're anxious, your stress mechanism's turned, changing many things inside your body such as disruption – particularly suppression – of your stomach's digestive function. When that happens, one of the undesirable effects is feeling nauseous or, worst-case scenario, you'll puke.
- Hard Muscles: No, I'm not talking about being fit and muscular. I'm talking about muscles that are chronically tensed. This is because your body turns on its fight-or-flight mechanism whenever you're anxious. This fight-or-flight mechanism preps your body up to take off or defend itself quickly by tensing the muscles unconsciously. It's like preparing to lift a barbell or sprinting in a relay race.
- Parched Mouth: Your mouth dries up due to anxiety due to several reasons. When you're anxious, you tend to – however unconscious – breathe through the mouth and the air passing through it dries up the saliva. Another effect of anxiety is acid reflux, which also dries up your mouth by hampering your salivary glands' ability to produce enough saliva to keep your mouth moist.

Anxiety Disorders' Effects On Your Body

Anxiety disorders are no laughing matter because they can seriously impact your life. For one, such disorders puts your body in a chronic state of hyper drive and stress that greatly increases your risks for some of the most serious health problems like high cholesterol, diabetes, short-term memory loss, digestive system problems, heart disease, heart attack and weakened immune system.

Anxiety disorders can significantly increase your risk for diabetes, especially if you have a sweet tooth. It's because stressful situations tend to make people, you included, eat sugar-laden foods just to be able to cope. And because anxiety disorders tend to put your body in a chronic hyper drive state, you tend to burn more calories, which make you feel you need more energy and fast. And guess what types of foods and drinks can help energize you fast? That's right – sugary foods!

The same goes for your risk of high cholesterol levels. This is because anxiety disorders tend to over-stimulate the sympathetic nervous system into releasing specific types of hormones that may lead to higher risk of increased cholesterol levels.

Anxiety disorders can also compromise your body's ability to digest the foods you eat. Why? It's because anxiety, being primarily a mental activity or state, heightens your brain's activity and in the process, makes it slow down your body's other important functions, which include digesting the stuff you wolf down. This increases your risks for digestive problems like diarrhea, bloating and indigestion.

Anxiety disorders can also make you resemble Dory, that adorably forgetful fish in the hit movie Finding Nemo, which was released in 2003. In the movie, Dory had short-term memory loss, which looked very cute and adorable on her. However, the only thing that anxiety will make you resemble Dory is the forgetfulness part, not the cute and adorable parts. Why? Anxiety heightens your cortisol levels (a stress hormone), which can seriously affect your mental performance, particularly memory and recall.

Your chances of getting the sniffles and cough, among others, also increase with anxiety disorders. It's because this condition – if chronic – tends to mess with your immune system over the medium to long term primarily due to cortisol it produces. And with a compromised immune system, expect to get sick more often.

Lastly, anxiety disorders can increase your risks for heart diseases. This is because it can result in chronically elevated heart rate and blood pressure, both of which further increases your risk of dying, especially due to a heart attack.

How Anxiety Can Impact Your Social Life

Social anxiety and phobias will get in the way of your relationships and social interactions. What would otherwise be fun and enjoyable moments can become moments of terror and panic, which can among other things, isolate you from most of the world.

How Anxiety Can Ruin Your Chances For Success

To succeed in life, you'll need to take risks. The greater the success you want to experience, the higher the risk you need to take. Anxiety disorders, however, lower your risk tolerance by magnifying the risks significantly more than the potential rewards. With risks seemingly becoming more imminent and much greater than the potential rewards, you may be inhibited from even trying to succeed.

Is There A Cure For Anxiety Disorders?

Well, there is good and bad news when it comes to curing anxiety disorders. Out of my exceedingly optimistic and kind heart, I'll give you the bad news first: No, it can't be cured. So the next time a huckster comes up to you offering a cure for anxiety disorder for the unbelievably low price of your life savings, it's time to kick some butt and bust some face. It'll make more sense to believe in the fat-loss claims of those home shopping network gadgets than it is to believe that there is indeed a cure.

Having done away with the bad news, are you ready to know the good one? Here it is: You can effectively manage it so that it won't interfere with your ability to live life to the full. Yes, you can manage it so well and minimize it that it no longer becomes a disorder.

In chapters 2, 3 and 4, I'll explain what is social anxiety as a particular form of anxiety disorder, the reasons behind such a disorder and the things that you may be doing that aggravates such a condition, respectively. The rest of the chapters – from 5 to 9 – will be about how you can effectively manage social anxiety disorder for personal success.

Chapter 2 – What Is Social Anxiety?

Social anxiety disorder used to be termed as "social phobia" and it is more common than we have ever been led to believe. Literally millions of people, across the entire globe, suffer from anxiety disorder, a traumatic and devastating condition, on a daily basis. For some, it may be caused by a specific social anxiety, for others it could be more generalized.

According to research in the United States, social anxiety disorder has been listed as the third biggest psychological disorder, following alcoholism and depression and the research estimates that about 7% of the population currently suffers from a form of social anxiety disorder.

People with social anxiety are generally described as having a very high level of shyness. We all feel a bit shy or nervous at times but some people feel it more extremely. For these people, it can be very debilitating. It affects their ability to go out and socialize, to meet new people, to get involved in new things. It may even start to affect their ability to go to work or school.

Some of the situations that can trigger feelings of social anxiety include:

- Speaking in public
- Speaking with people in authority positions
- Speaking with or to a group of people, even an individual at times
- Eating a meal in a public place
- Any situation that is performance based
- Being criticized or teased

- Being made to be the center of attention
- Interpersonal relationships, romantic or otherwise
- Being watched while they are doing something

When they are placed in these situations, people with social anxiety disorder may experience any number of symptoms, many of them physical and all of them uncomfortable, including:

- A feeling of butterflies in the stomach
- Heart beating rapidly
- Excessive sweating
- Blushing
- Some people even have feelings of nausea
- Dry mouth and throat
- Trembling
- Trouble swallowing
- Muscle twitches, usually around the face and cheeks
- Intense fear

They will worry that other people notice what is happening to them and will be negative towards tem, unfairly judging them.

The easiest way to describe how a person who has social anxiety disorder feels is to say that they feel as though they are in the spotlight, being singled out for attention, and that everyone thinks the worst of them. They believe that they are no good in social situations that they are incredibly boring and have nothing of interest to contribute to a situation or conversation. After they have attended a social event of some kind, they will shred the event to pieces, picking up on and focusing only on areas where they feel they did badly.

This is why most people who suffer from social anxiety disorder avoid public places; avoid getting involved in social events if they can. If they have to be involved then they will stay out of focus, hide in the background and try not to draw attention to themselves if they can possibly get away with it.

Chapter 3 - What Causes Social Anxiety?

There are a number of different explanations as to what causes social anxiety disorder. Every person is different and every person is likely to have different triggers. Here I am going to go over the most common reasons why people might suffer with social anxiety:

Behavioral

There is a theory that suggests some people develop a social anxiety disorder because of things that may have happened in the past. You know that, if a child touches something hot, like an oven door for example, the pain would teach them that oven doors are something to be avoided because they get hot and they can hurt you. Similarly, social situations where you were made to feel humiliated, embarrassed or fearful could have an effect on how you feel in future social situations. You may be afraid that all situations will be like this and, as a result, you start to avoid them.

Thinking

Another theory lends itself to the thought that some people have a style of thinking that leads to social anxiety. Someone who is anxious in social situations will predict to himself or herself that they will perform badly and they will think that everyone is watching them, judging them all the time. People who are socially anxious will doubt their own abilities to blend in and join in, believing they are boring and that nobody wants to hear what they have to say. Thinking patterns like this automatically make what could be simple nerves into something far worse.

Evolutionary

Evolutionary factors may also play a part in social anxiety disorder. To understand this, remember that humans are a sociable race and we tend to enjoy being in company. Some people don't like to think that they may upset other people and don't want to end up being rejected so, for some people, the start of a social anxiety disorder is a simple fact of being over sensitive to negative evaluation. This may be why many socially anxious people do everything they can to upset other people and, in the long-term they do more harm to themselves.

Biological

There is also the suggestion that social anxiety disorder may have familial ties. Look back through your family – if someone else has social anxiety issues then there is a good chance that you may inherit their personality traits. Genetic makeup may play a bigger role in social anxiety levels than we really know.

Traumatic or Bad Experiences

When someone experiences something bad or traumatic, extreme distress can be felt at the time it happens. But it doesn't end there because that experience can leave its mark on that person. Some of the more common of these experiences that are reported as happening to socially anxious people start in their school years. Bullying is a prime example, or anything else that singles a person out to be odd, somewhat different, and unacceptable in the eyes of other people; all of these can contribute towards social anxiety throughout life.

The Demands of Life

When you talk to people who have social anxiety disorder, most will say that they have always had it while others will say that it started when they were teenagers or in their early twenties. Teenagers and young adults have a lot of stumbling blocks to get over, especially socially, when they start to gain their independence and begin to establish their role as an adult in the roles that society expects of them. Getting through these challenges is not easy and the patterns that these young adults develop may have an impact on their life in the future and make some things hard to deal with.

Stresses of the Present

There are two types of stress that are likely to have an effect on the level of anxiety that a person feels – significant moves that server to cut contact with colleagues, friends and/or family; and significant changes that have an effect on the way a person relates to others, perhaps a change in their job at work. These demand that a person adapts to a new situation quickly and takes up a great deal of energy when, in all likelihood, there is little to spare. Confidence has to be built up ad this is a time when old vulnerabilities are likely to surface.

How All of These Factors Work Together

Most problems have more than one potential cause and it can be hard to separate them. However, the likely causes of a social anxiety disorder can be split into two different categories – stress and vulnerability, Vulnerability is something that is deep seated; characteristics that make a person susceptible and they can be biological or psychological

– in some cases, a combination of both. Psychological factors usually come from things that the person experienced earlier in life. Stress includes any demands that are being placed on a person in their present day life and circumstances that may be having an effect on them at the time.

In all honesty, you cannot pinpoint one single reason why a person may suffer from social anxiety disorder. In truth, there will be many facets to the reason and, to be fair, it is probably less important to know what caused it than it is to know how to overcome it.

Chapter 4 - What Aggravates Social Anxiety?

For the most part, we are the only thing that prevents us from overcoming social anxiety. It is our thoughts and feelings that put a stumbling block up and stop us from moving forward, in many cases doing nothing more than exacerbating the problem. The following will give you some insight into what is stopping us:

Unhelpful Thoughts

Our own unhelpful thoughts make it difficult to overcome social anxiety. Socially anxious people have negative thoughts about themselves and their ability to cope in social situations. This serves to lower their confidence levels, which, in turn, makes it more difficult for them to get involved in situations. And that means that they don't give themselves the chance to test their social interactivity skills.

These kinds of thoughts also tend to have a damaging effect on people who are about to enter a social situation. The thought that they will perform poorly or will do something to upset someone tends to have an influence on the way they feel and, as a result, the way they interact with others. Following a social activity that person will then sit and analyze how they behaved and believe that they did everything wrong. Thus, it is easy to see how unhelpful thoughts can play a big role in stopping people from overcoming their social anxiety.

Avoidance

Many people with social anxiety disorder will go out of their way to avoid social situations and social contact in any format but if they really can't avoid it then they will stay out of the way and try to get out of it as quickly as they possibly can. While this is a somewhat understandable method of coping with social anxiety, it is also the biggest reason why these people find it so difficult to overcome.

By avoiding any social contact, they are denying themselves the opportunity for positive experiences that can go a long way towards proving that their unhelpful thoughts and feelings are wrong. And, the longer they continue to avoid social contact, the harder it is to face them.

Using 'Safety Behaviors'

Sometimes, socially anxious people will use what they call safety behavior to help them feel comfortable in social settings. Examples of this type of behavior include:

- Staying in the background
- Keeping quiet
- Staying close to people they know well
- Avoiding any eye contact
- Drinking for courage

Although behaviors like these can make a person feel a little better at the time, they are not really very helpful long-term strategies for dealing with social anxiety. Similar to avoidance, safety behaviors stop a person from proving that they can cope in social situation, simply because they are hiding behind something or someone, and tend to put their social success down to other factors. As a result, their confidence levels remain low and their social anxiety is still very much in force.

Increased Self-Focus

Socially anxious people tend to spend a lot of time focusing on themselves during social situations. Sadly, this is another big reason why they find it hard to overcome social anxiety. For example, they may be trying to work out if they are blushing or sweating, whether they are stammering or stuttering and, as a result, they are making things much worse. They hope that nobody notices, significantly overestimating just how visible their anxiety levels are and making themselves very self-conscious in the process. Plus, while they are focusing on themselves, they are not concentrating on the situation or the conversation and may come across as distant or uninterested. The fact that they are not concentrating makes it harder for them to join in, thus reinforcing their belief that they cannot cope in social situations.

Food And Drinks

Although anxiety is primarily a mental issue, it is also a nutritional one, to some extent. Why? It's because certain foods and drinks can aggravate the physical symptoms of social anxiety, which can make you more anxious and so on and so forth or it can interfere with the beneficial effects of other foods. It can create a vicious downward spiral into anxiety abyss.

Speaking of social anxiety aggravating foods, here are some of the foods you should minimize or if possible, avoid altogether:

- Sugary Stuff: Especially those that are chock full of refined sugar, these kinds of food can aggravate your social anxiety through a phenomenon popularly known as sugar crash. This happens when you eat a lot of simple carbohydrates – like simple or refined sugars – that causes a sudden spike in your blood sugar, to which your body reacts by secreting insulin. The insulin acts quickly to bring your blood sugar levels back down to normal but the problem is it often overdoes its job and results in low blood sugar instead, which makes you feel lethargic or even sleepy. This is called hypoglycemia and repeated sugar spikes and crashes stimulate the production of stress hormones cortisol and adrenaline, which causes or aggravates anxiety and panic.

- Caffeine: A well-known effect of caffeine, which is responsible for its ability to keep you awake and alert, is elevated heart rate and along with elevated heart rate is elevated blood pressure. Unfortunately, both are physical anxiety symptoms. Consuming coffee and other drinks with high caffeine content will make you experience symptoms that can either trigger or aggravate social anxiety such as nausea, restlessness, inability to sleep and agitation. If you believe you need it to be alive, alert, awake and enthusiastic all the time, it may be that you're suffering from chronic sleep deficit. As such, your best bet would be to get enough of it.
- Alcoholic Drinks: Despite the prevailing social notion that alcohol is one of the best relaxants ever known to man, the fact is it can actually worsen social anxiety symptoms. This is because alcohol has the uncanny ability to screw up your brain's serotonin levels – and it's this hormone that's key to mood regulation. And apart from mood sabotage, most alcoholic drinks also contain – surprise – sugar, which you already know to be a social anxiety-aggravating ingredient. Together, this Batman and Robin tandem of alcohol and sugar can lead to feelings of nervousness, confusion,

restlessness and dizziness – symptoms of or can worsen social anxiety.

Always keep in mind that even a gram of prevention really is much better a kilo of cure when it comes to managing your social anxiety very well. As such, it's best to watch what you eat and drink for tomorrow you may not be merry due to social anxiety.

Chapter 5 – Instant Hits For Quick Social Anxiety Relief

"Handle every stressful situation like a dog. If you can't eat it or play with it, just pee on it and walk away." – Anonymous from Pinterest.com

No one is exempted from experiencing panic or social anxiety at some point in life. The only things left for discussion are the intensity and frequency of such experiences. Why? As humans who live in an imperfect world, there will always be something that can make everyone of us feel uneasy or concerned.

Some causes of anxiety are quite petty like when we're rooting for our favorite basketball team who happens to have Andre Drummond[1] on the free throw line for two free throws that can either win or lose the championship game or when Lionel Messi is attempting to make a goal against one of football's best goalkeepers if not the best, Manuel Neuer. Some are a tad bit more serious like when you're in an open-microphone karaoke bar and you find the microphone was suddenly given to you, with your mouth still full of nachos, to finish the song I Will Always Love You by the late Whitney Houston while your only public singing experience is limited to singing the Star-Spangled Banner together with the rest of your elementary school classmates in your school's open quadrangle! And of course, there are some with really high stakes involved such as pitching your company's services to a major client, the success or failure of which will determine if you'll still have a job the next day.

---

[1] NBA player with the league's worst free throw shooting percentage during the 2014-2015 regular season.

Social anxieties that aren't diagnosed to be a chronic medical condition, such as the examples above, aren't as serious as diagnosed social anxiety disorders. That doesn't mean however, that you shouldn't take them seriously. It's because like in the last example above, it may cost you something important and keep you from living life to the full.

Social anxieties can be managed well – you can enjoy quick relief – when you experience them every now and then. In this chapter, let's look at different quick and practical ways you can win over your social anxiety episodes.

Nothing

That's right, that wasn't a typographical error. Neither are you experiencing an OTBE or out-of-the-body experience. One of the best ways to quickly deal with your social anxiety attacks is really, just do nothing, which is actually oxymoronic because by consciously trying to do nothing, you're actually doing something here. Oh well, whatever. The point is just do nothing apart from doing nothing. Here's why it works for many people.

Consider your anxiety to be a bonfire on a cold winter night. If you want the bonfire to go away, you don't actually need to do anything but let it be. After some time, the bonfire will die a natural death for as long as no additional wood or flammable material is added to it. You simply starve it to death.

And that's what this tactic is about – starving the anxiety beast to death. You deny it the opportunity to grow healthy, big and strong. You may not know it but there are many ways that you think you're killing anxiety while in fact you're really feeding the monster:

- Avoiding social situations that make you feel nervous or anxious;
- Denying that you are nervous and anxious;
- Forced relaxation, which isn't really relaxation to begin with;
- Putting in more effort to ensure perfection at what you're doing instead of being excellent;
- Tensing our muscles unconsciously of course;
- Trying too hard to banish negative thoughts from your mind; and
- Waiting for – and hoping that it exists – the right moment to smack your fears on the noggin' and kill it.

There's nothing wrong in doing something for quick anxiety relief and as I'll show you later on, there are things you can do that will help. But there are many instances wherein doing nothing is the best solution, especially when you find it difficult or impossible to not over-apply well-known quick relief tactics for social anxiety.

Don't Breathe Too Much

Yes, as much as breathing is good, nay necessary, overdoing it can aggravate social anxiety. Remember how we talked about one of the symptoms of anxiety – feeling like you can't breathe? Breathing in too much air – also known as hyperventilating – can make you feel as if oxygen is in such short supply despite breathing more than your usual supply of the stuff. And often times, the normal reaction is to breathe in more gulps of air either by taking even deeper breaths or breathing much faster as if panting, both of which actually aggravate the situation even more.

But how can breathing too much air lead to feeling there's less of it in our lungs?

Geeky professor mode...ON!

The reason lies in how our bodies make use of all that air – dirty or otherwise – that we breathe in. Our bodies need sufficient amounts of carbon dioxide in order to process or obtain oxygen that's transported in our blood. And who would've thought that waste product we breathe out is actually necessary to process oxygen, eh?

What happens when you breathe in too much air is that there's so much oxygen for your body's normal carbon dioxide levels to process. In fact, doing so can even reduce the amount of necessary carbon dioxide in your body as you breathe more of it out due to the excessive oxygen amounts. With less carbon dioxide in your body, the amount of oxygen your body can process out of the available supply also decreases, hence the feeling of shortness of breath despite breathing in more air.

Feeling like you're going to die from shortness of breath is one surefire way to fan the flame of your social anxiety attack. And breathing in more air – as the natural response might be – only pours more gas on it. That's why you shouldn't breathe too much when feeling anxious. Just breathe normally, that's it. I'm not talking about deep belly breaths – just your normal, regular breathing.

Then you starve the anxiety beast.

It Too Shall Pass

Another way of managing the social anxiety beast – particularly non-chronic ones that aren't medically considered as disorders – is to simply acknowledge its existence and that its existence is just like the craze about Miley Cyrus' scandalous twerkings – temporary. When you do that, you empower yourself to let it be and rob the social anxiety situation of its power to wreak havoc in your life.

To make it more relatable, allow me to share my previous experience with this tactic within the context of my marriage.

There were times when my wife takes leaps of faith by risking the prospect of another sleepless night by letting me know something that I am doing wrong. And even though often times I react with peace and harmony in the beginning, it escalates when my wife – with the best of intentions – continues to prod at why I did it or why I continue to do it. After I explain (more like justify, hehehe) at the end of each prodding-round, she would prod even more until all my patience and understanding is used up and it becomes an argument.

Then an epiphany hit me one time - I figured, why not just acknowledge what I did wrong, that it was wrong and simply tell her I'll eventually be able to arrest it with her help. Guess what, it worked! Whatever tension built up in the beginning quickly evaporated. There were even moments where tension didn't even arise, however small.

By acknowledging what I did wrong as wrong, taking up the cudgels for it and believing that it's manageable and will eventually be rectified, I allow a situation to run its naturally quick course en route to its swift death. In many instances, it's the same with social anxiety in that it merely wants to be acknowledged. And like a reasonable person, it goes away after getting that which it wanted.

So how can you let non-chronic social anxiety moments run its naturally quick course? Simply believe it's like a strong thunderstorm in the Sahara desert – quick and temporary. Be aware that physiologically speaking, it's just a temporary adrenaline and cortisol rush that will subside as quickly as it flooded your system. In many cases, all it takes is several minutes to subside.

Another way of letting your non-chronic social anxiety episodes run their naturally quick courses is by accepting the realities of its triggers' existence and that its potentially ill effects are very minor in most cases – nothing life changing. For example, if its your turn to report the company's monthly financial performance to the Board of Directors, don't resist or judge it as either positive or negative. Simply acknowledge that yes, you will have to do it sooner or later and that given your bosses assigned you to do it means you have what it takes to successfully pull it off. If ever you make a mistake, it'll probably be very minor and non-consequential.

Talk To Yourself

While most people find this practice to be either odd or worse, crazy, it's one of the best ways to experience relatively fast relief from non-chronic social anxiety episodes. Despite the lack of any clear scientific evidence, many people believe that what we speak, our subconscious minds take as reality and thus act on that perceived reality.

If this were merely quack-science, why is it that there are tons of books – both physical and electronic – on the subject matter? One of the oldest books in the world already wrote about the power of self-talk. The Bible says in Proverbs 18:21 that the power of life and death is in our tongues. The Kindle Store best-selling book CEO Yourself by Rita Monroe extols the virtue and power of how we talk to ourselves and its ability to help us succeed in life.

Aside from convincing ourselves into calmness, talking to yourself also has the extra benefit of drawing our attention away from the cause of our anxieties. In a sense, it's another way of starving the beast, albeit indirectly, into dying a quick and natural death.

How do you actually talk to yourself without looking, sounding or feeling like a looney? Well, there are different ways to do it. The key thread that ties all these different ways together is positively assertive and not passive aggressive, the former being telling yourself what you want to feel and the latter telling yourself what you don't want to feel. In social anxiety situations, you should tell yourself that "You're calm and relaxed" (positive assertive) instead of "I'm not anxious and stressed", which is passive aggressive. For clarity's sake, passive-aggressive self-talk is denying how you really feel.

The 3 ways you can talk yourself out of social anxiety episodes is through problem solving, distracting memories and affirmations. Let's start with affirmations.

Affirmations are the most popular of self-talks and are positively assertive statements like:

- I am on top of this anxious episode;
- I may be anxious but I'm more powerful than my anxiety; and
- Because I'm much bigger and powerful than my anxiety, I function normally despite.

If you find that after the first application, you're still anxious about a social situation, don't despair, especially if it's your first go at it. Just continue talking to yourself in a relaxed manner without exerting to much effort and over time, this will be an effective social anxiety episode ender.

Another way to talk to yourself for social anxiety relief is by using distracting memories. Here, you simply tell yourself about your most favorite experiences and most joyful memories. One good thing going for this kind of self-talk is that it's based on something that's already happened, giving it traction in your mind and heart. And because of its joyful emotional links, it can be a very powerful agent for experiencing fast, non-chronic social anxiety relief. Instead of telling yourself that you want to be calm in this room full of strangers, you can tell yourself about the time when you felt comfortable in similar situations in the past or how calm and peaceful you felt when you were lying on a hammock at the beach.

Just because distracting memories have the benefit of proof doesn't mean affirmations are useless. No, there will be situations where affirmations will be more appropriate and effective than distracting memories and vice versa. With sufficient application, you'll be able very good at knowing when and where to apply the two.

Lastly, you can simply solve math problems or other verbal puzzles verbally. The benefit of this approach is distracting you enough until the anxiety beast dies its quick and natural death.

Familiarity Anxiety

Avoiding familiar ones, e.g., friends, places, looks to be a really bad idea at first glance. I mean, why on earth would you go to unfamiliar people or places to overcome social anxiety episodes? Wouldn't unfamiliarity aggravate your social anxiety?

No, not really. This tactic is consistent with the starving the beast strategy. How? Running to familiar people and places act like security blankets, especially during uncomfortable moments. This has the often-overlooked effect of feeding the beast – empowering it even! It's because by doing so, you suggest to your subconscious mind that yes, you can't overcome your social anxiety and its trigger on your own...that you need to depend on others, be they people, places or situations.

So the next time you feel like you want to run into the arms of familiar people, places and situations as a means of overcoming anxiety...don't! Simply stay put, relax, breathe normally, speak to yourself and simply allow your anxiety episode to just starve, sputter and die a natural death. Your chances of experiencing quick social anxiety relief are higher when you do this instead of running to the comforts of your security blanket.

Chapter 6 – Self Help Tactics For Managing Your Social Anxiety

The instant hit techniques enumerated in the previous chapter are, as mentioned, meant for isolated social anxiety episodes that aren't medically classified as a chronic disorder. There are times, however, that such social anxiety episodes tend to be much more frequent and for such cases, you'll need more than a Band Aid-like approach. There are 2 ways to do this: self-help or professional help. In this chapter, we'll take a closer look at the first one.

Thankfully, there are several self-help tactics that we can use to overcome social anxiety, including:

- Worrying for anxiety relief;
- Know if the anxiety trigger is solvable;
- Banishing unhelpful thoughts;
- Reducing internal focus in social situations;
- Minimizing or stopping the use of avoidance and safety behaviors; and
- Cultivating relationships.

It isn't helpful to try and do everything at once so, let's take things slowly and work through this one step at a time:

Worrying For Anxiety Relief

One unorthodox tactic for effectively coping with and managing social anxiety is to worry regularly. Yep, you read that right – worry regularly to effectively manage anxiety! Why on earth should you do that? Here's why: Do you know that regularly worrying is a good way to minimize the effects of social anxiety? Here's an illustration of how it works.

My wife and I love to ride our fixed-gear or fixie bikes. You know, those bikes with only one gear that doesn't allow you to coast and doesn't have brakes. Regularly riding those seemingly suicidal machines allows us to release all the pent-up energy from doing mostly intellectual work, which often times makes us fidgety and restless. As we expend the excess energy, we find that we are able to concentrate better on our work because the fidgety and restless feelings disappear or are significantly reduced to the point that they don't interfere with our work.

Since we live in an imperfect world, there are times that biking regularly isn't feasible or even possible. If such periods of time extend to more than what's reasonable, we tend to become agitated, restless and fidgety, which significantly affects our ability to concentrate on our highly mental occupations.

We try downplaying the effects, but there are just some things in life that don't go away by simply downplaying. This is one of them. We had to accept it's an integral part of our mental health and performance.

Knowing that, we do our best to take the time and ride our fixie bikes at least once a week for 45 minutes or its equivalent spread over the whole 7 days. I get to do the latter by biking to work everyday. My wife does it differently but the bottom-line is, we both do our best to get our regular weekly rides in for optimal mental performance.

You can do something similar for your social anxiety: set aside time to regularly "worry". This can help you in your efforts to effectively cope with and manage chronic social anxiety episodes in the long run.

But how does worrying regularly help you worry less?

One way is that worrying on purpose helps you meet your personal worry "quota", which helps you get it over and done with by the time you need to be calm and relaxed. It's like doing what you can now and not procrastinating. You let worry run its quick natural course at the most convenient time – when you're not doing anything that can be affected by your worrying.

Another way this helps is by what I call the Buffet Effect. No, I am not talking about Warren Buffet but a buffet lunch or dinner. When you stuff yourself with so much of your favorite food, usually at a buffet, you become so satiated that you no longer want it. It's the same – by worrying regularly at the most opportune times, you can make your mind feel so satiated with "worrying" that it can no longer stand to worry as much as you used to. You simply tire yourself out by worrying regularly.

Another way that regular worrying helps you manage social anxiety much, much better is by conditioning your mind to postpone it to a much better time of the day, say on your commute home from work. You're actually training your brain to police your social anxiety and put it in its proper place. You may not be able to eliminate it but at the very least, you put it where it doesn't do much damage, if any.

Lastly, a possible way that this works is that you simply make yourself too immune to anxiety, much like playing electric guitar frequently helps you build callouses on your finger tips and makes it perfectly painless to play guitar for hours on end compared to when you first did so. You also build up your mental strength and stamina for it like when you gradually increase your running distance or the weight of your bench press.

Now that we established that worrying regularly can be good for managing your social anxiety, how do you exactly make time for it? Well, it's really a no-brainer. Simply do it as you would make time for your favorite activity like eating, exercise, book reading or TV watching. Just do it at your predetermined time and place. Over time, being able to hold of social anxiety becomes much easier knowing that you have that time of the day to actually indulge in it.

What about social anxiety episodes at the most inopportune times of the day? Simply write down what's making you socially anxious at that time, put the paper in your pocket and go back to it later during your regular "worry" time.

Know If The Anxiety Trigger Is Solvable

I so love math when I was still studying. In fact, I love it so much that I am now doing work that's not anywhere near using math. Yeah, baby!

Seriously speaking, mathematical problems can be classified into solvable and not solvable. There was a time where I spent more than half of the allotted time to answer a specific, mind-boggling problem, which I never got to finish anyway. Because of my cramming habits back during my college days, I wasn't able to comprehensively cover all of the lessons prior. To my chagrin after the exam, my classmates told me that problem was simply not solvable or has no solution! If only I had known, I could've topped that exam and graduated as batch valedictorian...in my dreams.

Seriously, there's a lesson to be learned there somewhere when it comes to managing your social anxiety. Wait, I'm looking for it...oh there it is! The lesson is: If you know before hand if what's causing your social anxiety is something that you can address or solve or not, you can act accordingly. If the idea that people may not like your speeches gives you enough heebie-jeebies to experience a panic attack every time you come to events where you regularly do so, knowing that you really have no control over how people will perceive your speeches and that there will always be a person or two who won't like your speeches can free up your mind and help you relax. If the trigger is something you can actually do something about, then you can also relax knowing you can actually do something to minimize the trigger. Either way, it helps you to manage your social anxiety much better.

There are 2 ways to know if your social anxiety trigger is something you can solve or not. First, ask if you the trigger or problem is a real or imaginary one? Often times, you'll realize that your social anxiety triggers aren't actual problems or concerns but are merely all in your head. For example, it's much easier to banish the thought of being jeered at the financial management seminar you'll be conducting tomorrow when just yesterday, you were in the newspapers because you were given a prestigious award for being voted as the best finance manager by a leading business publication.

The other way to find out if the trigger can be solved or addressed is by asking if you're in the position to actually do something about it? For example, you may be worried about being ridiculed by the person you want to introduce yourself to at a prestigious business networking cocktail. Knowing that the reaction of the person is beyond your control, you can be set free from the obligation to worry about the results and focus instead of what you can control – the decision to take the opportunity to expand your business contacts.

Now that you know how to determine if the trigger is solvable or not, what's next? It's easy, simply discard the problem or trigger if it isn't solvable. It's the only choice really. But what if it is?

Just because it is doesn't mean you have the obligation to fix it immediately – whether immediately or later on – or worry about it until the cows come home. An example of this would be, say, the worry or fear that the person you want to introduce yourself to at that business networking cocktail will ask you to solve a very complex statistical problem to prove your worth as a business contact. Is that solvable? Yes, by Googling about how to solve such problems and mastering it in the next 30 minutes or before that person leaves. By doing so, you can actually help manage your social anxiety particular to that person. But should you actually do it?

One way to find out is to ask yourself: Is it productive? In this case, would it be worth the worry, cramming and missing out on establishing other new business contacts just for this person? Obviously, it isn't. So even if it's solvable, it isn't something worth worrying about or taking responsibility for whether now or later on. When you realize these things, you'll be surprised at how calm and relaxed you can be afterwards and how effectively you can manage your social anxieties.

Banishing Unhelpful Thoughts

We know that the way we think will have some kind of impact on our social anxiety and social successes. If you walk into a situation full of confidence, you will breeze through with flying colors, but if you go in feeling shy or that you are no good in social situations, you are going to struggle. Therefore, it is very important that we remember these barriers are only thoughts and thoughts can be banished. Tell yourself that your thoughts have no real basis, no real standing or meaning and are certainly not a fact. Question every thought you have and challenge it. Talk about how you can change the way you think. If you think about something in an unrealistic way, ask yourself what the basis for your feeling is. By doing this, you will eventually start to see things more realistically and that will help to reduce your social anxiety.

Patterns Of Unhelpful Thinking

You must first be able to recognize that you are having an unhelpful thought before you can challenge it. Most unhelpful thoughts follow a pattern and being aware of that pattern can help you to be more aware of when you are having these thoughts. Some of the common patterns are:

Predicting the Future

Socially anxious people spend a good deal of time thinking about what is going to happen in the future, predicting what is going to go wrong, instead of just letting it go. Most of your predictions will never happen and, instead you have wasted a lot of time and energy on it for nothing.

Mind Reading

You are assuming that other people are thinking bad thoughts about you, that they are talking about you when, in actual fact they probably haven't noticed anything different about you. All this does is lower your confidence and your self-esteem, making the situation far harder to cope with.

Taking Things Personally

Socially anxious people tend to take things very personally. If someone around you is quiet, it doesn't mean you have offended him or her in some way, you haven't done anything wrong, but you will automatically assume you have.

Over Generalizing

You may find that, because of one incident that happened just one time, you assume that all similar situations are going to end the same way. Just because one presentation went wrong, it doesn't mean that all future ones will. The chances are it was a one off and everything else will be just fine.

Focusing on the Negatives

Socially anxious people spend a lot of time dissecting social situations and looking for the bits that they think went badly. What you won't do is focus on any positive parts of the situation, looking solely for the bad in everything.

There are things that you can do to learn how to challenge unhelpful thoughts once you have recognized that you are having them. You must ask yourself some questions with each thought. Let's take a situation where you are about to meet some work colleagues of a friend of yours.

First of all, you will feel a little edgy, perhaps self-conscious and you will think that you will have nothing good to say and they'll think you are just an idiot. To challenge that thought, ask yourself what evidence is there of this? Tell yourself that you coped just fine in previous similar situations and you never struggle to find something to say normally so why would you this time?

What you are actually doing here is predicting what is going to happen. You are assuming that things are not going to go well but you can't say why you think that. Ask yourself this – what would your friend be thinking if he or she knew that his was how you felt? They would probably laugh and tell you that you were worrying over nothing, that you are good company to be in and that you will be fine.

Step 3 – Confronting the First Situation

Now that you have your list, or hierarchy, and you are happy with the order that it is in, it's time to start confronting the situations, one at a time. The first situation is the one that has or that you predict will cause you the least amount of social anxiety. While you are tackling this it is vital that you:

- Remember your anxiety levels will raise to start with but, if you hold out and stay put, it will drop.

- Remember that there is nothing wrong with feeling anxious. It is a natural reaction, perfectly healthy and we all feel it at some point in our lives. Yes, it can be an unpleasant experience but it is not a dangerous one and it will pass if you give it, and yourself, a chance.

When you face the situation you have chosen from your list, try to remain in it until your anxiety level has dropped by at least 50%. Let's say, you go into a situation and your anxiety level rises to 50 on the scale. Try to stay put until it has dropped to 25 or lower. How long this takes will vary, from person to person and from situation to situation. It could take up to 45 minutes, but is generally much quicker than that.

Be aware that some social situations do not allow you to stay in them for a long period and your anxiety level may not have a great deal of time in which to fall but that's OK. You can still take away from that situation a level of confidence that you didn't have before and that should make you feel more comfortable about other situations.

- Remember that anxiety is not as noticeable as you think.

- Don't use safety behavior or avoidance tactic – all these do is slow down what progress you are making. If you can't drop all of them at once, cut them out of your behavior one at a time

- Focus on the conversation and the people in the social situation. Do not focus on your own feelings, symptoms or performance, especially do not focus on what you think others are thinking about you

Do bear in mind that not all social situations can be predicted up front. You are bound to get caught in situations that happen out of the blue or by accident. A complete stranger asking for directions, for example, may approach you and you certainly can't really plan for that. Again, this is OK. If you do find yourself in that sort of situation before you are ready, just do your best and try to remember some of the tips you learnt earlier. Another thing you can do is be opportunistic. Look for situations that are coming up and prepare yourself for them.

Step 4 - Repeating the Exposure Task

Once you have faced the first task and completed it, do it again. And keep on doing it until you are comfortable in that particular situation and you no longer feel anxious, either thinking about the situation or being in it. Each time you confront the situation, your anxiety levels will drop just a little bit more and you will find it easier. Try to do it every day if possible but, if not, never leave more than a couple of days between otherwise you are giving yourself a chance to start that negative and unhelpful thinking again.

Step 5 - Moving Onto the Next Item on Your Hierarchy

You have done it; you have conquered the first task on your list. You should be very proud of yourself and you should be feeling might happy about now. You've taken the first step in beating social anxiety disorder and you should now be feeling a level of confidence that says you can move on to the next situation. So, on to the second one on the list and, don't forget, once you have done it once, keep on doing it, over and over again, until you are completely confident and not anxious at all. Do this for every situation on your list until you have reached the end. It doesn't matter how long it takes; there is no set time limit, it will take as long as it takes you to overcome your fear of social situations and regain your confidence.

As you progress through the list and your confidence grows, you should find it easier to tackle the higher anxiety level situations. Although you will still feel a degree of anxiety and fear, it won't be as bad as it would have been before you started this.

Trouble shooting

If you find that an attempt at facing a social situation does not go quite as well as you had thought it would, don't worry about it. This will happen and the easiest thing to do is to try again – but don't leave it too long before your next attempt. If it still seems as if it is going to be too hard to achieve, look at building an extra step or two before it on your list – perhaps you have under or overestimated other situations and you are trying to make too big a leap. Keep on pushing though, it will work and your confidence will grow again.

Cultivating Relationships

Although this tactic seems contradictory to that of avoiding familiar people and situations, it isn't. The kinds of relationships we're talking about here are those with people who can identify or relate to your social anxiety struggles. In other words, with people who are also managing or coping with social anxiety. Better yet, those who have already come to a point where their social anxiety no longer controls them.

Being part of a good support group can go a long way towards effectively managing and coping with your social anxiety. It can, for one, make you feel you are not isolated in your struggles with social anxiety. Knowing there are others like you who are going through the same or who have already experienced how it is to manage it well can give you the necessary encouragement and resiliency in the face of your challenges.

Another way that flocking with other birds of similar feathers is that you get to see, hear and learn first hand how to win over your social anxiety. Reading great resource materials can give you lots of theoretical wisdom but nothing beats witnessing how its done to fully appreciate and learn how to manage social anxiety.

Lastly, cultivating relationships is also fun because if you know you're with people who are also socially anxious, nothing can be more reassuring to you that you really won't be judged or criticized. In fact, you can even get to share and hear different stories and laugh together at what you are going through, making it a much lighter challenge to bear.

Mindfulness

Social anxiety isn't just feeling edgy or nervous – we all feel that way every now and then. A socially anxious person will experience unrealistically exaggerated threats, hyper-arousal, chronic negative thinking and powerful fear in social situations most people would find non-threatening or normal. Because these experiences trigger that person's fight-or-flight response system into high gear, social anxiety can also lead to the manifestation of significant symptoms like digestion problems, elevated heart rate, palpitations and high blood pressure. These symptoms may become very severe that it impedes a person's ability to function normally on a daily basis.

Cognitive-Behavior is one of the most popular professional treatment programs available for managing and coping with social anxiety. Also known as CBT, this primarily involves changing a person's thoughts in order to manage and cope with social anxiety. We'll get into more details on CBT in Chapter 7 on professional therapies.

Mindfulness is the practice of being aware of our feelings, thoughts, surrounding environment and bodily sensations moment-by-moment. This is another way you can cope with and manage your social anxiety. Unlike CBT, mindfulness is more concerned about changing a person's relationship with his or her thoughts instead of the thoughts themselves. When practicing mindfulness, a person focuses on bodily sensations that are felt during social anxiety episodes or moments. Rather than withdraw from or avoid those sensations or feelings, the person chooses to be "in the moment" and fully experience the social anxiety symptoms. And rather than staying away from negative thoughts, the person receives them in order to acknowledge and see such thoughts' inaccuracy or invalidity.

Although this practice seems counter-intuitive at first glance, it can be very helpful in terms of managing your social anxiety by helping you distance yourself from those negative thoughts. This happens as you practice the art of letting disruptive thoughts go as a way of responding to them instead of avoiding them, which in all possibility isn't doable. When you remain in the present, you'll learn that your social anxiety symptoms are nothing more than reactions to perceptions of being threatened. Responding to these thoughts instead of reacting to them can help you override that faulty fight-or-flight response system that kicks into high gear during social anxiety episodes.

A survey of 19 studies on the effectiveness of mindfulness conducted by Vollestad, Nielsen and Nielsen found that anxiety symptoms were significantly reduced through mindfulness. As such, practicing mindfulness can be as effective as CBT for way less money. They also found significant reductions in depression symptoms, which is interesting since depression is estimated to affect up to 40 percent of people suffering from social anxiety disorder. The survey concludes that changing the relationship between a person and his or her thoughts on anxiety can be help reduce feelings of distress.

Simply put, being mindfully anxious can be a good way to manage and cope with it. The more you realize that your social anxiety isn't an accurate perception, it'll lose its power over you.

So how can you use mindfulness to help you in coping well and managing your social anxiety? Here are practical ways you can do it.

Stay In The Moment

Often times, we pump ourselves up so much in preparation for social events by trying to recall many details about how things went such as if we offended someone with our words, how the atmosphere was during the event and how well did we handle ourselves during the event, among other things. The problem with those things is that they're not the moment – they're past.

Staying in the moment means knowing that this is a new event on a new day or evening. Part of being in the moment too is simply looking at events objectively, i.e., no judgments or evaluations. This includes not blowing things out of proportion even before they happen. Doing this tends to become a self-fulfilling prophecy of failure.

Learn To Radically Accept Things As They Are

Radical acceptance is a term that may be considered peculiar to the practice of mindfulness. It means to simply accept all feelings and thoughts with no judgments, regardless of how "bad" or "good" they seem. It's easy to be objective about thoughts that are more, well, objective. It's a different thing altogether when you talk about things that really scare the living daylights out of you.

The ability to really do this requires much effort and practice but it's worth the effort because it does help bring down stress levels and contributes to improving your sense of comfort and well being in uncomfortable situations.

Counter Talk

If a negative or anxious thought persists despite doing your best to radically accept them for what they really are, counteract the negative self-talk by asking yourself questions such as:

- Is there proof for this nagging anxiety thought's validity?
- Is this nagging thought always valid?
- Has this thought occurred or happened before?
- Seriously, what are the chances of this nagging thought coming true?
- What's the worst-case scenario for this and is it really that bad?

- Am I looking at the whole picture or just a piece of the pie?
- Am I being objective or emotional?

After asking yourself these questions, it's time to counter attack with positive affirmations or self-talk and writing them down can help a lot. Catching yourself engaging in negative thoughts and retaliating to them with supportive and positive affirmations concerning you, the chances of a mental turnaround becomes significantly higher. With enough regular practice, you'll empower yourself to change your thinking and emotions more consistently, particularly during social anxiety attacks.

For example, if you regularly experience anxiety attacks (fear of being ridiculed in public) prior to entering a room full of people you don't know, which continue to persist despite radically accepting such thoughts, simply ask yourself any or all of these questions:

- Are there any reasons for me to believe this fear?
- Has this fear materialized before?
- Seriously, what is the probability that this will actually happen considering it hasn't before?
- Is the worst-case scenario for this fear really that bad?
- Is this fear a myopic view or am I looking the whole picture?
- Am I being objective or emotional about this fear?

You can then counter by telling yourself that you're confident being around strangers and that there's no chance they'll ridicule you because these are educated, cultured and mannered people.

Think About Your Breathing

When you focus on your normal breathing (not hyperventilating, mind you), you are able to bring your focus back into the moment to ground you and remove your focus from anxious thoughts. Here's a good way to do this exercise:

- Put your hand over your diaphragm, feeling it expand as you inhale and contract as you exhale. Remember, don't hyperventilate – just breathe normally.
- As you do this, focus your attention on all the body sensations you may feel without evaluating or interpreting them.
- Continue focusing on your breath and relax when you exhale. Do this 10 times before repeating.

When you focus your attention on how you breathe, you calm your central nervous system, reduce your body's stress levels and lower your blood pressure. Doing so also gives you the benefit of being distracted away from whatever anxious thoughts or feelings you may be experiencing.

Scan Your Body

This activity is another integral part of the mindfulness practice. It allows you to pay close attention on each part of your body with no judgments whatsoever, helping you relax them. You can scan your body with eyes open or closed, sitting, standing or lying down. You can even do this while falling in line at the grocery counter or at the bank, while waiting for your doctor's appointment and even while having your haircut at the saloon! The cool thing about it is that it's not obvious you're doing it – at least it doesn't have to be.

Chapter 7 – Professional Help: Therapy

There are many cases where social anxiety disorders are managed and coped with very well with self-help techniques. And that's great. However, there are cases that are more serious and require the help of medical professionals in terms of managing and coping.

There are two types of professional help you can get for managing and coping with more severe cases of social anxiety: therapy and prescription medicine. While it is not my place to give professional advice on how to manage social anxiety, I can orient you on the common therapies and prescription medicines that licensed professionals will probably prescribe for you. It's my hope that this and the next chapter on prescription medicine will help clarify any misconceptions about professional therapy and medicine that you may have or simply help inform you in your decision to seek professional help.

In this chapter, we'll take a look at the common therapies for social anxiety.

Cognitive Behavior Therapy (CBT)

Widely believed to be the most accepted and most popular anxiety therapy all over the world, it has been shown to be effective in helping patients deal with anxiety disorders, including social anxiety, generalized anxiety, phobias and panic disorders, among other medical conditions. With CBT, people who suffer from social anxiety are taught how to address their wrong notions and harmful thinking patterns about themselves and the rest of the world as a means of coping with and managing their social anxiety.

As the name implies, its main components are cognition and behavior. The cognitive aspect, or cognitive therapy, is concerned with addressing the effects of undesirable or wrong thoughts (or cognitions) on a person's anxiety disorder. The behavioral aspect of the therapy deals with that person's reactions to and behaviors in particular situations or events that trigger or aggravate his or her anxiety disorder. CBT's underlying principle is that anxiety disorders – including social anxiety – are due to a person's way of thinking and not his or her personal external circumstances.

With CBT, the professional therapist assists you by helping you change the way you think by posing challenges to your undesirable or wrong thinking patterns. Such thoughts are believed to be the single biggest reason for anxiety disorders and as such, they need to be replaced by positive and healthy thoughts. This process can be broken down into 3 important steps: identify, evaluate and replace.

Identify

The professional therapist first helps the client identify their scary and irrational thinking patterns by asking them what was running through their minds when the anxiety disorder or attacks first started to happen. Often times, this can prove to be quite a challenge for both the therapist and the client because often times, clients aren't totally aware of when the disorder first started to manifest and what they were thinking at that time. But the extent to which this is identified is also the extent to which the therapy can help the client successfully manage and cope with their anxiety disorder.

Evaluate

After the undesirable or wrong thinking patterns have been successfully identified, the therapist assists the client in evaluating them and even challenging those thoughts. After the client has evaluated those thought patterns, the therapist challenges such thoughts and evaluations by asking for proof as to their validity, analyzing those though patterns and even determining the extent to which those thought patterns actually came to pass, i.e., how often they actually happened. The therapist challenges these thinking patterns by objectively assessing the chances of the anxiety trigger actually happening, weighing the pros and cons of either worrying about that trigger or avoiding situations, and experimenting.

Replace

The final part of CBT is where the professional therapist assists the client in removing those undesirable and wrong thought patterns with desirably accurate ones. The therapist can utilize realistic and calming affirmations to help the client manage and cope with their anxiety attacks and episodes.

Hypnotherapy

The use of hypnotherapy as a form of treatment for social anxiety disorders is relatively, it evolved from work that was done on animal magnetism by Franz Anton Mesmer, an Austrian physician from the 1700's. However, it wasn't until 1958 that hypnotherapy was recognized by the AMA (American Medical Association) as a valid medical procedure. Since that time, hypnotherapy has been used to treat a number of disorders, not just anxiety but also other chronic conditions that are linked anxiety, such as irritable bowel syndrome and asthma.

This type of anxiety therapy makes use of – surprise – hypnosis, which is defined as a process of bringing a person to a heightened awareness state (also known as a trance) by using intense concentration, focused attention and guided relaxation. Under this type of therapy, the main goal is to make the client focus on just one thing and exclude everything else – and I mean everything! When the client enters into a trance, the professional therapist, also known as – surprise – a licensed or certified hypnotherapist, is able to give suggestions to the client's subconscious mind on how he or she will positively manage and cope with their particular anxiety disorder and analyze the reasons for it.

When the client is in a trance or under a state of hypnosis, he or she becomes more open to discussions and suggestions concerning his or her anxiety disorder, which can greatly increase the chances of successfully dealing with or treating the anxiety, phobia or fear, among many other things.

Hypnosis, however, isn't for everyone. People under the influence of alcohol or narcotics are advised not to undergo hypnosis because their minds are not clear at that point.

Unfortunately, most people the same way the government is trusted by conspiracy theorists trust hypnosis. It's mostly because of how the media inaccurately portrays hypnotists as scheming con artists or worse, criminals. Truth of the matter is hypnosis is not dangerous because it isn't a form of mind control or brainwashing. Even under hypnosis, the hypnotherapist won't be able to make the client do something without their consent or permission.

How Does Hypnotherapy Work?

Hypnotherapy is based on the idea that certain events, things that have happened to us at some time in our lives, have become linked to both emotional and physical reactions. When we experience a particular event again, the emotional or physical reactions are reactivated, whether they are healthy ones or unhealthy.

As well as the actual hypnosis, a person may also be given a post-hypnotic suggestion, one that tells them they will find it easy to relax when they want to.

What Happens During Hypnotherapy?
Before you begin a session of hypnotherapy, the therapist will look at your medical history, they will discuss the problem that you are seeing them for and they will explain to you how hypnotherapy works.

During the hypnotic state, a person's blood pressure tends to lower, as does the heart rate and they will experience deep relaxation, accompanied by a change in brain waves. It is in this state that a person becomes open to suggestion. Each session should last between 30 and 60 minutes and, at the end, you will be brought out of the hypnotic state and back to being alert to reflect on what happened and how you felt.

Does Hypnotherapy Really Work for Social Anxiety Disorder?
At this stage, few studies have been done to assess the impact or hypnotherapy on anxiety. However, there have been controlled randomized trials carried out and these have shown that hypnotherapy can help to reduce anxiety and can also help to enhance the benefits of cognitive behavioral therapy.

Before you attend a hypnotherapy session, there are some things that you need to consider. First, although it is a rare occurrence, it is possible for some psychological problems to be made worse by hypnotherapy. For example, if you suffer from BPD (bipolar personality disorder), any dissociative disorder or have ever been the victim of severe abuse, you should make your therapist aware because hypnotherapy may not be the best course of action. As well, you should also attend hypnotherapy sessions only after receiving a diagnosis from a mental health professional. That is the only way to ensure that the hypnotherapy is being used in the right way to treat the right problem.

Chapter 8 – Professional Help: Prescription Medicines

Our thoughts and emotions are, at the very core, physiological in nature. Our brains produce certain hormones or chemicals that influence the way we think or feel about people, things and situations. So while psychological approaches to social anxiety disorders can yield meaningful success in many cases, there are still times when they're not enough and the solution lies in going physiological via prescription medicines.

Unfortunately, prescription medicines, much like hypnotherapy, have gotten a really bad rap these days especially from the all-natural and organic-is-the-only-way-to-go segments of society. They've crucified prescription medicines as if these were the reincarnations of the devil himself or at least creations of such reincarnations. While it's true prescription medicines have been abused many times and has lead to deaths, the problem isn't with the medicines – it's with the users who illegally and without prescriptions obtained and consumed them.

The key to successfully using prescription medicines for social anxiety disorders can be summed up in 5 words: prescribed by a health professional. No competent and trustworthy health professional will prescribe pills for social anxiety without first considering other non-medical ways of managing and addressing such. Medications should be the last resort.

Here are some of the common prescription medicines for treating not just social anxiety but anxiety disorders in general. The reason I'm discussing them with you is so that you can make informed decisions and ask your doctors the right questions if and when they prescribe these medicines for managing and coping with your social anxiety disorder. Remember, this is not in any way, shape or form a substitute for professional medical advice.

Tranquilizers

Anti-anxiety medicines are called tranquilizers. The most common kind of tranquilizer used for treating anxiety disorders are Benzodiazepines or Benzies[2] for brevity. These include:

- Ativan (Lorazepam);
- Klonopin (Clonazepam);
- Valium (Diazepam); and
- Xanax (generic name Alprazolam).

These anti-anxiety medicines are so effective that they can give anxiety relief within 30 minutes to an hour. If only for this reason, Benzies are the primary prescription drugs of choice for quick relief for extreme anxiety and panic attacks.

But as with most good things in God's green earth, it isn't perfect as it has some side effects ranging from irritating to serious. These include impaired coordination, sleepiness and brain fog, all of which can seriously affect your studies, work and critical daily functions like driving. Some people noted that it feels like having a wicked hangover the next day after a wild night of drinking. Other side effects of taking Benzies include:

- Clumsiness;
- Confusion;
- Depression;
- Emotional numbness;

---

[2] Benzies: A term I personally concocted to refer to the longer-named original version, particularly for my writing convenience. Consider it for your reading convenience too.

- Forgetfulness;
- Impaired thinking; and
- Sluggishness.

And oh, I forgot to mention some really serious side effects like:

- Aggressiveness;
- Hallucinations;
- Mania; and
- Rage.

Anti-Depressants

Also known as antideps, these medicines are primarily used to treat – surprise! – depression. These medicines include tricyclic anti-depressants (TCA), monoamine oxidase inhibitors (MAOI) and selective serotonin reuptake inhibitors (SSRI). In most cases, antideps are the preferred anti-anxiety drug by most doctors because of the lower risk of becoming dependent on the drugs or worse, abuse. The tradeoff for lower risk for dependency and abuse is quick relief. While Benzies can give you quick relief at the risk of dependency and abuse, antideps can take a while to kick in and give you relief. How long is "a while"? Well, between 4 to 6 weeks long. When your social anxiety disorder is kicking overdrive and you need real time relief, antideps ain't gonna cut it. And just like the Benzies, antideps have their own share of side effects such as:

- Headaches;
- Nausea;
- Nervousness;
- Sexual dysfunction;
- Sleepiness;
- Upset stomach; and

- Weight gain.

Oh, another issue that you'll need to consider prior to obeying your doctor's prescription – if he does prescribe this – is the possibility of experiencing withdrawal symptoms when you stop taking antideps, particularly if done abruptly. Personally, I didn't experience withdrawal symptoms when I quit on my antideps cold turkey but the general consensus among experts is that there is that risk. Consider me a mutant or a general aberration of the population that's why I didn't suffer withdrawal symptoms.

Buspirone

Also known as BuSpar, this is a relatively milder reincarnation of the deity called tranquilizers. The way it works for anxiety relief is that it increases your brain's serotonin levels and reduces that of dopamine. Given it's a kind of tranquilizer like the Benzies, it's not as fast in giving real time anxiety relief – it takes 2 weeks on average before relief kicks in.

Given it's much slower acting than the Benzies, it has its share of advantages. First, it doesn't sedate you as much as Benzies. Second, it doesn't impair your coordination and memory as much as its stronger siblings. Lastly, with lower strength come lower risks for dependency, abuse and withdrawal symptoms. But it still comes with side effects:

- Constipation;
- Diarrhea;
- Dizziness;
- Drowsiness;
- Dry mouth;
- Headaches; and
- Nausea.

Beta Blockers

Although this type of prescription drug is primarily taken for treating high blood pressure and heart problems, it's also used to help manage anxiety disorders. Beta blockers can help you experience anxiety relief by blocking the production of norepinephrine, a stress hormone that's primarily responsible for our fight-or-flight response system as well as helping control other anxiety symptoms such as voice tremors, elevated heart rate, dizziness and shaking hands.

More Caution

Regardless of the anti-anxiety prescription medicine, you should avoid consuming prescription painkillers, sleeping pills and alcohol because mixing them can prove to be fatal. If you're on anti-anxiety meds, you'll need to skip the anti-histamines too if you want to increase your chances of enjoying your newfound anxiety relief for a longer time.

Senior citizens, pregnant women and substance abusers (both recovered and recovering) should also avoid anti-anxiety prescription medicines. Senior citizens, due to their age and health, are much more sensitive to the side effects of these medicines unlike younger people. Even the tiniest dosages of such medicines can lead to confusion, amnesia, imbalance and symptoms of dementia – all of which can significantly increase their risks for accidents and injuries.

If you're pregnant and care for your child, skip these prescription medicines. It's because they can be transported to the placenta, increasing your unborn child's risk of suffering from sleeping problems, breathing difficulties, weak muscles and irritability after they're born. And even if you take them after you give birth, take note that these medicines can also come out together with your breast milk.

Final Word On Prescription Medicines

As much as prescription medicines are effective in providing you with anxiety relief, their documented side effects should make it your last resort for managing and coping with your social anxiety. And of course, it should only be done upon the prescription of your doctor.

Chapter 9 – Nutritional Tactics For Social Anxiety

How many times have you heard the saying that you are what you eat? To some extent, it is true. You eat healthy food, you become healthy. You eat garbage, your body becomes garbage. You eat foods that help you keep calm, you become calmer.

Eating the right foods can greatly increase your ability to manage and cope with anxiety well. Eating right includes whole foods, herbs and supplements.

Whole Foods To Enjoy

No matter how you put it, eating whole food is always healthier than eating processed ones, regardless how healthy manufacturers claim their foods to be. A great guiding principle as to evaluating how healthy – or unhealthy – a food item is: the Paleo Principle. This principle states that the closer a food item is to its original form, the healthier it is. So between a piece of apple and a slice of apple pie, it's clear which among the two is healthier.

Why is processed food inferior to whole ones? Most of the essential and beneficial nutrients of food are lost with so much processing, including cooking. Worse, some kinds of processing actually make foods unhealthy either by changing the food's molecular structure or by adding unhealthy ingredients. And if you want to be able to manage and cope with your social anxiety very well, you'll need all the nutrients you can get and minimize unhealthy ingredients as well.

In terms of coping with and managing social anxiety, or just about any anxiety disorder, the Mayo Clinic promotes several dietary practices. One of them is eating a breakfast that's high in protein. It's because eating protein makes you feel full for longer periods of time. It also helps you stabilize your blood sugar levels for stable energy the rest of the morning.

Another dietary practice the Mayo Clinic espouses is going for complex carbohydrates instead of simple ones. Carbohydrates can help you manage your social anxiety as it promotes more production of serotonin in your brain. As you learned earlier, higher levels of serotonin are beneficial for anxiety as it helps calm you down. Why complex carbs? It's because complex carbs help you keep a stable blood sugar level, which not only makes you more energetic and alert but also lowers your risk for diabetes. Those are 2 less things to worry about.

Drinking enough water daily is another healthy dietary practice the Mayo Clinic is pushing for coping with and managing anxiety. Dehydration can affect your mood in ways that may trigger your anxiety. As a general guideline, go for 6 to 8 glasses daily and don't wait for your urine to turn dark yellow in color before going for a gulp. By that time, you're already dehydrated.

The Mayo Clinic, as with all other nutrition experts, also push for eating balanced, healthy meals, which is also important for optimal mental health. In particular, load up on fresh fruits and veggies, and omega-3 fatty acids rich fishes like salmon and trout. Just keep in mind that even if you eat healthy and balanced meals, you should still be careful not to overeat.

Some of the best whole foods to eat for managing and coping with your social anxiety – or any anxiety disorder in general – include:

- Acai Berries: As with blueberries, this is another super food that's packed with phytonutrients and anti-oxidants.
- Almonds: Its high zinc content is one good reason to go nuts about this nut. Zinc plays an important role in maintaining a balanced mood, which helps reduce anxiety. It's also rich in iron, which is important because anemia can aggravate your anxiety by making you feel more fatigued than usual.
- Blueberries: This nutritionally dense super food packs a lot of phytonutrients, anti-oxidants and vitamins that can help fighting stress.
- Chocolates: Hallelujah! Yes, you read that right! Hold your horses though, I'm not talking about those highly processed and sugar-filled commercial versions like Cadbury, Snickers and Hershey's. I'm talking about sugar and milk-free dark chocolate – the purest form. Pure dark chocolates contain mood-improving compounds. It also helps bring down cortisol levels. Remember cortisol – a stress hormone?
- Seaweeds: A great whole grains alternative for getting enough magnesium and tryptophan.
- Whole Grains: This can be very beneficial for you but only if you're not sensitive to gluten. Whole grains are loaded with magnesium (not getting enough of which can aggravate anxiety), complex carbs for steady energy and tryptophan for producing the calming hormone serotonin.

Herbs

Besides making many of your dishes even more delicious, did you know that herbs can also help you with your social anxiety? One of the reasons is because they're all-natural and are thus healthy. Second, some herbs have anxiety management properties that can help. These herbs include:

- Lavender: Oil extracted from this herb was found to be as effective as a known anti-anxiety Benzie – Lorazepam – in managing persistent generalized anxiety disorder in a study done in 2010. The good part? It doesn't have the same sedative effects. How to use this? Start with 80 milligrams daily as aromatherapy for anxiety relief.
- Passionflower: Studies have shown that this herb works just as well as some Benzies for coping with and managing anxiety but – as with lavender – with less sedation, according to the University of Maryland Medical Center. It was also shown in another study that it helps reduce anxiety, agitation, irritability and depression in former opium addicts who are recovering. How to use this? Start with 90 milligrams of its liquid extract or a cup of passionflower tea 3 times daily.
- Lemon Balm: Normally used with other herbs, this herb can also be beneficial for managing and coping with anxiety on its own. In 2004, a published study was conducted that showed lemon balm (600 milligrams to be exact), made the study's participants more alert and calm as well as reducing their stress levels. How to use? Start by drinking tea made of 1 teaspoon of dried lemon balm up to 4 times a day.
- Chamomile Tea: This is one tea that doesn't stimulate you into being more alert but instead helps calm you down, making it much easier for you to cope with and manage your social anxiety disorder. It contains beneficial compounds that mimic the effect of another Benzie, Valium, that bind itself to your brain's

important receptors. In fact, a University of Pennsylvania study revealed after taking chamomile tea for 8 weeks, subjects' anxiety symptoms went down significantly.
- Hops: Sorry, this doesn't refer to the finished product (beer) but the ingredient itself. In particular, hop extracts can be used for aroma therapy n your pillows buy stuffing them with it. It's rarely consumed as tea due to its bitter taste.

Supplements

These days, it's practically impossible to get all of your daily nutrition requirements solely from food. It's because most agricultural soil these days are already fatigued, i.e., significantly reduced nutritional content, due to over-farming. In fact, the people from ages ago seemed to be wiser than us in terms of acknowledging soil fatigue. The Bible's old testament required the Jewish people to let their agricultural soil rest for one year after every 7 years by not planting anything on them.

Another reason for not being able to get all our nutritional requirements from whole foods – particularly veggies and fruits – is storage and transportation across great distances. Long storage periods tend to remove most of foods' minerals and vitamins, particularly Vitamin B-complex and C.

Finally, heating food also leads to nutrient destruction, particularly cooking at high heat. As eating raw foods that aren't named sushi and sashimi are unpalatable to most people, it's highly unlikely that all nutrients can be obtained from eating whole, raw foods.

Do you want to know how impossible it is to get all your recommended daily allowance (RDA) of essential vitamins and minerals? Consider Vitamin E, the RDA of which is roughly 30 IU or international units. For you to get this much from food everyday, you'll need to eat:

- 10 pounds or on average 40 ears of fresh corn;
- 2 pounds of wheat germ;
- 3 pounds of almonds;
- 33 pounds of spinach; or
- 50 pounds of broccoli.

When you consider the impossibility of eating that much food in one day, consider too the fact that this is just for Vitamin E alone. How about all the other important Vitamins and minerals? I can tell as early as now that if you tried it, your tummy would explode!

Now that I've made the case for supplements, here are some supplements that may help you cope with and manage your social anxiety well:

- Gamma-Amino Butyric Acid: Also known as GABA for brevity, some evidence exists concerning its ability to help improve relaxation. As such, it's believed to help in managing anxiety symptoms.
- Kava: This is the most common and popular anxiety management supplement in the market. It's also possibly the one that has the most scientific backing. Studies revealed that it can stand toe-to-toe with some of the more common anxiety prescription medicines in the market. Even as a supplement, it's much like the prescription meds in that it doesn't mix well with alcohol, along with other prescription medications. Also, you may do well to avoid this if you have a history of liver illness or an alcoholic, either recovering or still one. But even if you're in the clear and this isn't pharmaceutical grade stuff, you'd do well to get your physician's clearance first.

- Magnesium: It is widely believed that not getting enough magnesium can either result in or aggravate anxiety symptoms like panic disorder or social anxiety. This is because magnesium is an essential mineral for healthy nerves, which can affect anxiety levels.
- Melatonin: The supplement form of this sleep-inducing hormone that's naturally occurring in your body is regarded as an anxiety management aid with good potential. It's because it's relaxing effect on your body may help relieve some of your anxiety. Take caution though, melatonin needs prescription in some areas so make sure you have one if you're in a place where it's needed. Also, it can make you fall asleep against your wishes, particularly in higher dosages. As such, make sure you start with half of the smallest dosage possible to gauge tolerance.
- Passionflower: You can also get this herb in nutritional supplement form. Although not as potent as Kava, it doesn't react to alcohol and is still generally beneficial for managing anxiety levels.
- Valerian Root: The supplement form of this sleep inducing herb can help you relax, which is good for managing your social anxiety. In fact, some studies have validated it's ability to help improve symptoms associated with anxiety.
- Vitamin B12: As with magnesium, this vitamin is essential for a healthy nervous system. Some studies also showed that supplementing your diet with Vitamin B12 can help improve anxiety symptoms.

Supplementary Caution

Despite not being considered as pharmaceuticals and hence, no prescriptions needed, you would do well to consult first with your physician prior to taking these supplements. Better safe than sorry as these can impede your ability to work, study or do other important things, especially if you're suffering from a medical condition or are taking other prescription medicines or supplements. Prevention is always superior to cure.

How to Create an Anti-Anxiety Diet

We cannot place the blame for anxiety on food but what you eat and how you eat does play a part in how you cope with anxiety. Some foods are "designed" to create the symptoms of anxiety while others can help you to fight those symptoms.

The truth is that diet really does matter but it is a vicious cycle. Many people who feel anxious will eat comfort foods to make them feel better. But the food you eat has a direct effect on the way you feel and the levels of anxiety you feel – high sugar, high carb foods make you feel better, but only for a short while, while other foods release certain feel-good chemicals into your body. Getting the balance right can be a very valuable tool in helping you to cope with the symptoms of a social anxiety disorder.

We've all hear the term "eating healthier", it's one that is thrown around quite a bit these days but, when it comes to anxiety, eating a healthier diet really does make a difference. Filling your plate with vegetables will fight your anxiety symptoms way better than a plate full of unhealthy burgers,

The way to create an anti-anxiety diet is to remove certain foods – those that could very well be contributing to your anxiety symptoms. The following foods should be removed or, at the very least moderated:

- **Fried food** - these are extremely difficult to digest, have very little in the way of nutrition in them and also contribute to the risk of heart disease. If your body cannot properly process the food you are eating you will struggle to fight off anxiety symptoms

- **Alcohol** - many people with an anxiety disorder turn to alcohol in the mistaken belief that it will make everything better. It does not. Aside from the fact that too much can make you do stupid things, alcohol does not do your body any favors. It is dehydrating, throws your hormones off balance and knocks out your nutritional balance as well. And the toxins that are going into your body can cause physical anxiety symptoms.

- **Coffee** - Caffeine is a stimulant and, in moderation, it will not cause any issues with anxiety symptoms. However, the more of it you consume, the worse your risk becomes. Coffee also causes your heart to beat more rapidly as well as other sensations that can lead to panic attacks. Limit your intake to one cup per day.

- **Dairy** - Dairy products are not actually bad for you, so long as you consume them in moderation. Large amounts of dairy can cause your adrenaline levels to rise and that can contribute to heightened anxiety. Cut down the amount you eat and, if you find that eating dairy is causing your symptoms to worsen, cut back again or cut it out altogether.

- **Refined Sugar** - While the sugar in fruit is not bad, the sugar in desserts is. In the same way that caffeine does, sugar stimulates the human body to produce a certain shakiness that can help to exacerbate any of your anxiety symptoms.

- **Food That Form Acid** - Yoghurt, eggs, pickles, wine, sour cream and liver all create acid in the body and there is a very good reason to believe that these foods also reduce the levels of magnesium in the body as well. Low magnesium is one of the contributors to or causes of anxiety, especially in those who already have an anxiety disorder so cutting these foods back or out altogether is a wise decision.

While avoiding these food types is not going to cure you of your anxiety disorder, it can certainly help, especially if you find that you eat too much of one or more of them. You don't have to eat a rabbit food diet; most foods can still be eaten but moderation is the key here if you want to help yourself to reduce anxiety symptoms. Remember this – a body that is nutritionally sound is more able to fight off the symptoms than one that has been filled full of junk foods.

6 Foods That Help You to Fight Anxiety

So, you know which foods to avoid but do you know which ones to eat more of? The following foods can help to reduce the symptoms of anxiety. Eating a healthy diet helps your hormones to function properly and that leads to an overall sense of wellbeing. Try to include these foods in your diet:

- **Fresh Fruit** – Your body needs a certain amount of sugar and carbohydrates but it doesn't need the refined ones. Fresh fruit contains natural sugars that are converted into energy and burned off. They also contain nutrients that are necessary, including vitamins and antioxidants. Blueberries and peaches are two of the very best.

- **Vegetables** - Vegetables are even more important than fruit especially if you have an anxiety disorder. Most vegetables contain high levels of fiber and are packed full of vitamins, especially those that are rapidly depleted in those with anxiety disorders.

- **Water** - Most people are dehydrated because they do not consume anywhere near enough water. Dehydration puts the body into an anxious state and that can make it much harder to fight off the symptoms. Aim to drink at least 1 ½ to 2 liters of water per day.

- **Foods Rich in Tryptophan** - These foods have been proven to be highly effective at helping to reduce the symptoms of anxiety. They include a component that helps you to relax naturally and can also help to increase your metabolism, which is always a bonus. These foods include poultry, soy, sesame seeds and oats.

- **Foods That Are Rich in Magnesium** – around 25% of the population is deficient in magnesium and that is one nutrient that has a large role to play in the human body, Magnesium is involved in more than 300 different processes in the body and it is crucial that you get sufficient amounts. Foods like tofu and black beans are rich in magnesium.

- **Omega-3 Fatty Acids** – While research into omega-3 fatty acids is still ongoing, we do know that is a vital nutrient for anxiety and depression. You can get omega 3's from fatty fish, like salmon and mackerel, winter squash and flax seed.

Chapter 10 – Complementary and Alternative Treatment for Social Anxiety Disorder

Complementary and alternative treatment is one of the fastest growing approaches to health care, fully backed up by vast amounts of scientific research and evidence. Complementary treatment is used, as the name suggests, alongside traditional treatments and the most commonly used one is aromatherapy used as a way of reducing pain and discomfort following major surgery. Alternative medicine is used instead of conventional treatment, for example, the use of a special diet as a way of treating cancer, rather than opting for surgery, chemotherapy or radiation treatment, which would normally be recommended by a member of the medical profession.

Treatment for Social Anxiety Disorders

At this moment in time, the following alternative and complementary treatments are used to help treat social anxiety and depressive disorders:

Relaxation and Stress Techniques
Relaxation techniques can produce short term, somewhat modest reduction in anxiety in people who have ongoing health issues, like inflammatory bowel disease or heart disease, those who are undergoing breast biopsies, dental or other medical procedures. Relaxation techniques have also been shown to be useful in adults with anxiety, more specifically the older adults. In those who have generalized anxiety disorder there are studies that show CBT cognitive behavioral therapy) may be more useful and effective in the long term than relaxation. For people who have the symptoms of depression, relaxation techniques may show a modest

benefit but are nowhere near as good as or as beneficial as CBT or other psychological treatment forms.

Relaxation techniques are considered to be an important part of many treatments for anxiety disorder, most specifically, social anxiety disorder. An example of this is those who have a genuine fear of public speaking, a fear that paralyses them, makes them stutter and struggle. Deep breathing and muscle relaxation are two techniques that can be practiced while the person imagines himself or herself standing up in front of a large group of people and speaking. There are four main techniques that may be used in the treatment and all of these can be practiced for any kind of anxiety.

Diaphragmatic Breathing

Otherwise known as deep breathing, this is the art of learning to expand your diaphragm when you breathe. This is to make your stomach rise and fall, not your chest and the reason why this works is because, during an anxiety or a panic attack, you tend to take short shallow breaths, which only adds to the anxiety symptoms. By learning how to breathe deeply and slowly in a setting that is relaxed, you will be able to bring it into action whenever an anxious feeling or a time of stress overtakes you. It is important to learn this technique because all the other relaxation techniques are built with deep breathing as the basis.

How to Practice Diaphragmatic Breathing

- Get yourself into a comfortable position, be it standing, sitting or lying

- Lay your hands, one on your stomach and one on your chest

- In order to maximize your intake of oxygen, you must learn the art of belly breathing, or breathing deeply from your abdomen. Focus your attention entirely on your breath until you can feel your stomach rising and falling significantly more than your chest every time you inhale and exhale.

- Breathe in deep through your nose and hold the breath for several seconds

- Exhale the breath through your mouth. The time that it takes you to exhale should twice as long as it took to inhale. One pattern that you could get into is the 4:7:8 pattern – inhale for 4 seconds, hold the breath for 7 seconds and exhale for 8 seconds.

- Do this 4 to 8 times, up to three times daily

If you find that you are struggling to focus on your breathing, think about using a simple phrase or movement that is repetitive to help you. One research group in Italy use two groups of participants in a study and asked each group to repeat a bit of the rosary or a yoga mantra six times in a minute, corresponding with the natural fluctuations in the circulation system. Both groups found it much easier to synchronize their cardiovascular patterns and increase their intake of oxygen.

Progressive Muscle Relaxation

If you are one of those people who works out hard, think about this – have you ever noticed how you feel when you have just finished a workout? Your muscles are fatigued to the point that your entire body is relaxed and this is the object behind PMR – progressive muscle relaxation. Alternating between relaxed and tense muscles can help to induce a full body relaxation.

Progressive muscle relaxation was first introduced by Edmund Jacobsen, an American physician in the 1930's. The technique is used as a way of reducing anxiety by alternating the tension and the relaxation in all of the major muscle groups in the body.

People who suffer with social anxiety disorder most likely have tense muscles most of the time. By practicing progressive muscle relaxation, you learn to have a better control over the way your body responds to anxiety. It is normally used as a complementary therapy with behavioral therapy techniques like systematic desensitization. However, it can be used alone. If you practice this right, you could end up falling asleep in which case, well done, because you have achieved a deep enough level of relaxation.

If you suffer with any kind of medical condition, you must consult with your doctor before doing any relaxation techniques

How to Practice Progressive Muscle Relaxation
- Find a place that s quiet and free from distractions
- Lie down on the floor or lay back in a chair
- Loosen off nay clothing that is tight and take off glasses or remove contact lenses
- Have your hands resting your lap or on the arms of the chair
- Take a few breaths, slow and even. Practice your diaphragmatic breathing
- Focus all your attention of your forehead, squeezing the muscles in the forehead for about 15 seconds. Make sure the rest of your body is relaxed and only the forehead muscles are tensed
- Feel those muscles tightening up and tensing

- Now count slowly for 30 seconds and release the tension slowly. Feel the difference between your tensed muscles and relaxed muscles. Continue until your forehead is completely relaxed
- Next focus on your jaw, tensing and holding the muscles for 15 seconds
- Release to the slow count of thirty second
- The neck and shoulders are next. Raise your shoulders to your ears, increasing the tension and holding for 15 seconds. Release for the count of 30 seconds
- Draw your hands slowly into a fist and pull your fists in towards your chest. Hold for 15 seconds. Release the tension and count for 30 seconds
- Increase the tension in the buttocks for 15 seconds and then release the tension slowly for 30 seconds
- Increase the tension slowly in your legs, concentrating on the calves and quadriceps. Squeeze as hard as you can and then release over 30 seconds
- Lastly, the feet. Increase the tension in your feet and your toes slowly and tighten up the muscles as hard as you can. Slowly release over 30 seconds and notice the tension slipping.

As you do this, concentrating on one part of your body at a time, notice how all your tension disappears, melting away as if it were butter left out in the sun. Enjoy the feeling of complete relaxation that takes over your body and continue breathing slowly, deeply an evenly.

Autogenic Training

Autogenic training is a technique that is similar to that of meditation. Under autogenic training, you will repeat statements to yourself, about particular parts of your body and the repetition of these statements is thought to influence how your autonomic nervous system functions. And this includes your heart rate.

Autogenic training was first introduced in 1932 as a relaxation technique by A Germany psychiatrist called Johannes Heinrich Schultz. He noticed that people who underwent hypnosis went into a state of relaxation where they experienced heavy warm feelings. He wanted to recreate that in a way that reduced anxiety and tension. It is thought that, by repeating a series of statements about warmth and heaviness in parts of the body, the autonomic nervous system is affected in a positive way. Although it isn't quite so well known as a relaxation method as other methods, a study carried out in 2008 found that autogenic training was efficient in treating anxiety. With social anxiety disorder, autogenic training can help to relax a person and to help in the reduction of symptoms when used as a complementary treatment, especially in terms of relaxing and calming a person in social situations and performance related situations. Practiced often enough, the words "I am calm" could be sufficient to bring about a state of relaxation at the time you say them.

Again, if you suffer from any psychiatric or medical conditions, you should consult with your doctor before beginning this, or any other, relaxation technique. Autogenic training is not to be used if you suffer from severe emotional or mental disorders. If you do start to do this, you should stop straightaway if you experience extreme anxiety, restlessness or any other effects that cause an adverse reaction, either during or after the training.

How to Practice Autogenic Training

Find somewhere that is free of distraction and quiet. Get into a comfortable position and remove glasses or contacts. Loosen off any clothing that is tight and rest your hands on the arm of the chair or in your lap. Take some slow, deep and even breaths, breathing from your abdomen,

Practice saying the following statements quietly:

- Say to yourself, "I am completely calm."
- Now focus on your arms and say to yourself, "My arms are very heavy." Say this 6 times
- Follow this by saying "I am completely calm."
- Focus on your arms again and say, "My arms are very warm." Say this 6 times
- Follow by saying, "I am completely calm."
- Focus on your legs and say, "My legs are very heavy. Say this 6 times.
- Follow by saying, "I am completely calm"
- Focus on your legs again and say, "My legs are very warm". Say this 6 times.
- Follow by saying, "I am completely calm"
- Say to yourself "My heartbeat is calm and regular. Say this 6 times
- Follow by saying "I am completely calm."
- Say to yourself, "My breathing is calm and regular". Say this 6 times
- Follow by saying, "I am completely calm."

- Say to yourself, "My abdomen is warm." Say this 6 times

- Follow by saying, "I am completely calm."

- Say to yourself, "My forehead is pleasantly cool." Say this 6 times

- Follow by saying, "I am completely calm."

- Enjoy how the relaxation makes you feel, the warmth and the heaviness. Revel in it and embrace it.

- When you ready, say to yourself, "Arms firm, breathe deeply, eyes open."

Guided Imagery

How many times have you wanted to escape, to leave it all behind and head for some warm tropical island or lock yourself away in a log cabin on a snowy hillside? Not many of us actually have the time, let alone the money, to fulfill our deepest wishes but you can do the next best thing – guided imagery. This is a technique that involved the use of all senses to visualize yourself in a completely relaxed setting. Once your mind is there, your body will follow and enter into a state that is fully relaxed. Do be aware that this can send you to sleep so do not do it when you have to be somewhere! The best time to do this is at night, just before or when you go to bed.

The use of guided imagery for relaxation is a good technique for those that have social anxiety disorders. Some of the most common things that people imagine or visualize are the sounds of the sea washing up on a sun kissed Tropical Island, or curled up in front of a huge, roaring log fire while the snow settles outside. The idea is to come up with a scene that relaxes you, not what you are told to imagine. It really does not matter what the scene is; what is important is that you "experience" every sound, every smell and every sight, that you transport yourself to that place when you close your eyes.

Once again, medical advice must be sought before trying this if you have a medical condition.

How to Practice Guided Imagery
We will use the popular beach setting for this but, when you try it, imagine your own personal place of relaxation.

- First, find a place that is quiet and free of distractions

- Remove glasses or contacts and loosen tight clothing

- Rest in a comfortable position and place your hands on your lap or resting on the arms of your chair

- Next, take some deep and even breaths, directly from your abdomen

- When you feel that you are relaxed, close your eyes and picture a white sandy beach. You are lying on this beach, surrounded by sand, swaying palm trees and crystal seas lapping at the shore.

- The sky is cloudless above you, you can feel the heat of the sun warming your body

- Breathe in deeply and smell the tropical flowers and the salt of the ocean

- Hear the waves rolling in and the birds chattering in the trees around you

- Feel the sand, warm and inviting, beneath your skin and notice how fresh a tropical fruit drink tastes

- Stay there for as long as you need. Notice how much

calmer and more relaxed you are and enjoy that feeling as it spreads own your body, from the top of your head, to your fingertips and the tips of your toes

- Notice how far away those feelings of stress and anxiety seem

- When you are ready, count from 10 backwards to 1 and slowly open your eyes. You will feel alert but totally relaxed at the same time

Meditation

There is some evidence to suggest that meditation can be used successfully to help relieve the symptoms of anxiety and depression, especially in adults. Mindfulness meditation is growing fast as an addition to traditional treatments, such as medication, and to other complementary treatments of social anxiety disorder, such as cognitive behavior therapy.

Most people, when you mention the word "meditation" to them, automatically think of sitting on the floor, legs crossed, closed yes and chanting the same phrase repeatedly. While some forms of meditation do involve this, mostly concentrative meditation, mindfulness meditation is far more open.

History of Mindfulness Meditation

Mindfulness meditation is firmly based on Buddhism and its roots are firmly in Sen and Tibetan meditation. It first became popular in the United States when a psychologist by the name of Jack Kornfield became a co-founder of the Insight Meditation Society in 1976. Since then, the popularity of the practice has increased, with the help of experts like John Kabat-Zinn and the development of a program for stress treatment. Mindfulness meditation is the core component of this program and, since it began, it has also been used as a complementary treatment alongside ACT (Acceptance and Commitment Therapy. It has also been incorporated into other psychotherapy models, like DBT (dialectical behavior therapy).

What is the Goal of Mindfulness Meditation?
The ultimate goal of mindfulness meditation is to develop an awareness of experiences, internal and external. Instead of using analytical thinking or emotion to react to events or thoughts, you will learn how to disengage your responses and regulate them. For example, if you were about to give a speech and you noticed that your hands were beginning to shake, mindfulness meditation can help you to avoid the panic and stop it from spiraling out of control. You be aware of the anxious symptom but you would pay it much heed and would not react to it. Mindfulness meditation has been shown to help with balancing emotions, increasing relaxation and in regulating behavior, as well as liberating you from automatic reactions.

How Does Mindfulness Meditation Work?
Mindfulness meditation works by changing your thought processes, your attention and your awareness. It trains you how to be aware of and to observe your emotions and thoughts without actually reacting to them. Over time, you will be "de-conditioned" to the extent that you can experience negative emotions and negative thoughts without reacting negatively and without trying to understand them. You will break the connection that exists between your anxious thoughts and your panic symptoms and you will train your mind to behave differently.

When it is used as part of a therapy treatment plan, mindfulness meditation is directed at a specific concern such as negativity in your way of thinking, or the physical anxiety symptoms. Research show that taking part in an 8-week course is effective in lowering the symptoms experienced with panic and anxiety. Mindfulness meditation is useful in treating social anxiety disorder, because it can act on a number of different areas – attention, thoughts, awareness, behavioral patterns, psychological responses, spirituality and relationships.

During the therapy, mindfulness meditation can be used as way of increasing how aware you are of the issues you experience and the helps to change how you react and how you respond. In general, it is used as a way of cultivating a stronger awareness, better self-control, and a better ability to regulate emotional reactions.

You can use the following mindfulness meditation script to help you to overcome social anxiety disorder. The script has been based on a basic meditation and is aimed at people who suffer from anxiety.

- Find a quiet place that free of distractions, choosing a time when you know that you can be alone

- Set a timer for anywhere between 20 and 40 minutes, to signal the end of the meditation – this is a typical length of time

- Begin by seating yourself comfortably – sit in a chair with a comfortable but alert posture, your back straight, your feet flat on the floor and your hands resting comfortably in your lap

- Ensue that you are balanced and are not straining to maintain your position

- Loosen any clothing that is tight and shut your eyes

- Gradually become aware of how still your body is
- Relax your chest, your stomach and your shoulders and start to focus on your breathing
- Breathe deeply, in through the nose, allowing the air to go down to your diaphragm and then release it
- Repeat, letting the air flow through
- As you breathe out notice how calm you feel
- As you start to find a comfortable breathing rhythm, feel the tension and the stress flow out of you
- As you breathe out, become aware of any thoughts or feelings that you have. If your mind wanders, if you start to worry about things that have happened, or things that may happen, this is normal
- Some of these thoughts may be distressing but try to observe them and not judge.
- Note the feeling or the thought and what it is about – perhaps an upcoming social event or a conversation that you feel could have gone better.
- If you find your attention grabbed by a negative feeling or thought, note it and then focus on your breathing again
- Try not to criticize yourself
- Notice the feeing but do not follow it and, most importantly, do not allow your mind to go after it
- Recognize that it is only a thought, notice it and then let it go
- Picture yourself lying on the beach on warm sand. The

breeze blows refreshingly over you, you can hear the waves rolling in to the shore and you feel your body relaxing

- Concentrate on your breathing, imagine it to be like the waves and the wind

- Remain calm as the wind blows over you and the wave's roll in; let your thoughts move and change at will. Breathe

- Now you must bring a situation to mind intentionally; a situation that brings on feelings of anxiety. Imagine yourself in that situation and keep the uncomfortable thoughts in your mind. Relax, let them float off but do not resist them. Simply accept and let them dissolve

- You cannot expect anxiety to disappear completely so do not resist it; accept, let it come, welcome it and then let it go.

- Count for 15 seconds; allow your brain to begin strengthening and establishing new paths.

- The more those paths are used, the deeper the groove and the easier it will be to fill them with happier thoughts

- When you are ready, bring your attention back to your breathing

- Move your attention to your body and then to your surroundings

- Open your eyes and stretch

Yoga

Yoga combines the use of meditation, physical posturing, breathing exercises and a distinct philosophy. Studies have shown that practicing yoga and other physical forms of exercise can help to reduce the heart rate, the blood pressure and can also help to reduce the symptoms of depression and anxiety.

Regular yoga can help to keep you calm and relaxed as you go about your daily life. It can also help you to find the strength to face up to events as they happen without feeling restless or anxious. Practicing yoga to the greatest benefit involved the use of asanas, which are body postures, pranayama's, which are breathing techniques, meditation and the philosophy of ancient yoga. It has been shown to help those with social anxiety disorder to carry on with their life in a relaxed and stronger way, with a more positive outlook on life.

The following techniques can help you calm you mind and say hello to a new and positive you. The best way to do this is to go to a yoga class and learn the techniques properly.

- Use asanas to get your body moving and free your mind of stress. Learn how to do these yoga postures to remove tension and negativity from your entire system:
    - Dhanurasana – the Bow Pose
    - Matyasana – the Fish Pose
    - Janu Shirsasana – the One-Legged Forward Bend
    - Setubandhasana – the Bridge Pose
    - Marjariasana – the Cat Stretch
    - Paschimottanasana – the Standing Forward Bend
    - Hastapadasana – the Standing Forward Bend

- Adhomukha Shwanasana – the Downward Facing Dog
- Shirshasana – the Headstand
- Shavasana – the Corpse pose

When you have completed the session of asanas, or yoga poses, lie down in the Yoga Nidra and give your body and mind a chance to relax. This is helpful in flushing toxins from the body, one of the biggest causes of stress.

- Use pranayama's to breathe properly and relive anxiety. By concentrating on your breath, you can free the clutter from your mind, get rid of the negative thoughts that cause anxiety, Learn the following pranayamas:
  - Kapal Bhati Pranayama – the Skull Shining Breathing Technique
  - Bhastrika Pranayama
  - Nadi Shodha Pranayama – Alternate Nostril Breathing – this is highly effective for stress relief because the exhalation is longer than the inhalations
  - Bhramari Pranayama – Bee Breath

Follow this up with meditation to free your mind. This is an excellent way of relaxing your mind, of freeing it from distractions and providing you with a sense of peace and of calm. Observe daily how your mind works, how it keeps you involved in concentrating on small and petty things, and stop concentrating on the things that cause you anxiety. It can also help you not to brood on the future, to worry about what might happen.

I have no doubt that you have heard the term "adrenaline rush". This is what happens to us when anxiety sets in, when you become worried about a particular threat. Let's say that you are about to step onto a thrill ride at an adventure park. At the tie, the adrenalin hormone in your body peaks and that leads to a fast heartbeat, your muscles tensing up and profuse sweating. Scientific studies have shown that, if you take part in regular meditation, you can reduce how much of this hormone is actually produced.

Next, you must learn the ancient philosophy of yoga and apply it in your everyday life. The principles are simple yet profound and they are the secret to a long, happy and healthy life, The Santosha principle will teach you the strong value of being contented while the Aprigrah principle can help you to put aside feelings of greed, the desire to have more possessions, both of which lead to anxiety and stress. The Shaucha principle talks about mind and body cleanliness and this is a useful one if one of the causes of your anxiety is the thought of infectious disease.

Lastly, we come to prayer. This is absolutely the best form of support and the reassurance you need to remain free of stress and anxiety. Developing a daily prayer habit will fill you with positivity, energy and will help your mind to calm and be still Prayer instills a sense of confidence, positivity and calmness instantly.

Think about how you can help other people instead of becoming rooted in the "me and mine" state of mind. Helping others can help you to relieve stress and anxiety, as well as making you feel much happier.

Banish negative people and situations from your life. Keep yourself surrounded by positive happy people and you will find that your mind is lighter, happier and your whole attitude towards life will be different.

Chapter 11 - Homeopathic Approach to Social Anxiety Disorder

Left untreated, social anxiety disorder can lead to several other psychological disorders. A homeopathic approach can be adopted and may be helpful in all areas of this disorder by using a holistic approach to look at each person individually. Each person has their own personality and this is derived from their genes, how they were brought up and their background. Being able to enforce a mental calmness means the potential to revitalize longevity, dynamism and wellness.

Homeopathic remedies are to be taken alongside a healthy diet and lifestyle to help make your mind and emotions healthy again. It's no good trying these remedies if you don't make the changes in other areas of your life. Homeopathy can help to enrich your mental health, can boost the way you function in social situations and remove the markers for anxiety by providing you with a sense of calm and peace. It can help you to overcome phobias, overpower your anxiety and give your self-assurance a much-needed boost.

One note about homeopathy – these remedies are all-natural and can be used alongside traditional medications. They are not potent, they are not toxic and they are not habit-forming or addictive. Below, we look at some of the more common homeopathic remedies that can be used in your fight to subdue social anxiety disorder. Although these are natural remedies, please make sure you seek the advice of your doctor before starting any of them.

Ambra Grisea

This is one of the best remedies for people who suffer from agoraphobia to the extent that they go numb with fear at the thought of going out. They absolutely dread meeting people, want to be left alone all of the time and cannot physically do anything while other people are around or near them. People with this form of anxiety are not able to express themselves and have to put in a lot of effort to take part in any conversation. They are very self-conscious, worrying constantly about how others see them and what they think of them, of their habits and the way they work. People who suffer this badly are usually anemic, weekend and don't sleep well.

Argentum Nitricum

This is a highly functional remedy used in the treatment of people who are very nervous. They may experience absolute fear at the thought of meeting new people, of speaking in front of people and may get very shaky. They may experience spasms in the throat and tongue muscles, distorted senses and shaking throughout the whole body. They are highly emotional, very hesitant and lack confidence. They are fearful, either faltering when they speak or not being able to talk at all. They may falter in their gait, they suffer with a fear of impending doom, can't bear darkness or crowds. Their actions can be seen as irrational and neurotic. This is a good remedy for people with anxiety disorders to take before they attend a big event, such as a social gathering, an interview or a public speech.

Baryta Carbonicum

This is used to great effect in individual who suffer with a real lack of confidence, are very shy and have few to no friends. They may be very confused, will have a fear of meeting new people and will grieve over small things. They may experience aphonia, which is an ability to produce a voice and they will very dependent in relationships. They can easily be suppressed because they will fear arguments and will be very aloof, highly inhibited and will believe that people are talking about them or laughing at them. This will stop them from going out because they will fear being in public places.

Ignatia
This is a good remedy for people who are emotionally sensitive and who will lose the ability to speak after experiencing a traumatic event. They will very likely suffer with hyperesthesia to all of their senses, a very heightened physical sensitivity, and their coordination will be somewhat disturbed at times. They will be alert and very apprehensive about everything, highly sensitive to the point of hysteria at times, very easily excited and will be quick to perceive things, usually believing that others are against them. Because of this, they will close themselves off, brood quietly and exhibit extreme mood swings. They will also reject any company without any communication.

Lycopodium
Sometimes known as just Lyc, this remedy has been shown to provide relief to those who suffer with an anxiety disorder that results in a real lack of confidence and very poor self-esteem. Although it can be used by people who have generalized anxiety disorders, it is best used by people whose anxiety comes on very quickly, without warning, usually in social situations. It will be accompanied by a whole host of physical symptoms, like a very rapid heartbeat, nausea, trembling and sweating. Many of those who use Lycopodium find that it stabilizes their emotions and their nervous system to the extent that they are able to cope better and experience less physical or emotional symptoms.

Aconite
Aconite has been in use for many centuries as an herbal homeopathic remedy for anxiety and panic. It is very useful for those people whose anxiety symptoms are as a result of

insomnia or another sleep disorder that cause nervousness. It is also helpful for those who suffer with irrational fears that come about for no apparent reason. Aconite has also been used for many years as a homeopathic treatment for hysteria and a number of phobias because it has a very calming effect on the brain. It is frequently recommended for use in treating mood swings, restlessness and nightmares.

Passionflower

Passionflower is the homeopathic remedy you are most likely to have heard about. It is the most popular herbal remedy used for treating anxiety and panic and it is often recommended by holistic practitioners as part of the treatment for panic attacks. If you are a person who suffers with panic attacks then you know just how debilitating they can be and you know what negative effects they can have on your life and on the people around you. There have been many studies that have looked at the beneficial properties of passionflower but the best was one that was carried out in 2011 in Norway. A study took place on 200 subjects and it was determined that blends of herbal remedies that contained passionflower showed benefits akin to those seen with medications such as Xanax, Ativan and other similar benzodiazepines. However, if you are taking any of the prescribed medications, you should not take anything that has passionflower in it without first consulting with your doctor or any licensed healthcare practitioner, as the combination could have the result of very excessive drowsiness.

Gelsemium

Gelsemium is a very effective homeopathic remedy of those who suffer with an anxiety disorder that causes constant jitters. While a low level of anxiety is nowhere near as debilitating as panic attacks that come on suddenly, any degree of chronic anxiety is not pleasant to live with.

Gelsemium is also known as yellow jasmine and it works to slow the nervous system down and calming the mind without causing excessive sleepiness. This is a good one to use when you are in a social situation, at work or anywhere where anxiety symptoms may strike you

Evening Primrose Oil

This homeopathic remedy has been used for centuries as a medicinal herb. It is one of the most effective remedies used in the treatment of all types of anxiety disorder. If your symptoms include chronic nervousness, panic attacks or social anxiety, you will find many benefits in using Evening Primrose Oil. This is because the oils has a nutrient in it called gamma linoleic acid. This helps to improve the function of the nerves and stabilizes the hormones. It is more commonly used to treat mood swings that are associated with premenstrual syndrome and menopause. You may need to use it regularly for at least three weeks before the benefits become fully clear.

Although most of the herbal remedies available do not have any, or at least very few, side effects, it is wise to consult your doctor first, before you add it to your daily diet. It is also wise to check whether the homeopathic remedy will interact in a negative way with any prescription medications you may be taking.

These are just a few of the remedies available but all of them can help you to reduce the symptoms of your anxiety disorder quite significantly.

Chapter 12 - Using Thought Records for Social Anxiety Disorders

Thought records, also known as thought diaries, are commonly used in the treatment for social anxiety disorder. They are a way for people to understand their negative thought patterns and to change them. The cognitive-behavioral therapy model works on the premise that behaviors and emotions can be changed because they are partly as a result of your own thoughts. Albert Ellis, a psychologist came up with the ABC behavior model:

- A – an activating event
- B – triggers thoughts and beliefs
- C – that result, in turn, in consequences

It may seem to many people that their feelings are directly attributed to certain situations, but you may be surprised to learn that there is another step between the situation and the resulting emotions. That step takes the form of your own thoughts. Perception plays a large part in determining how you feel about a person or a situation and, for most of us, the thought process is so automatic that we don't even realize that we have had certain thoughts.

Let's just imagine for a minute that you are at a party and you are chatting away with someone when he or she yawns. Depending on your particular thoughts about the yawn, your feelings will be different:

- If you thought that the person was rude to yawn, the chances are you will feel annoyed
- If you thought that the yawn was meant to signify he

person was bored with you, you might feel somewhat bad about yourself

- If you thought that the yawn was telling you the other person was tired, there's a good chance that you will be indifferent

Just one single event can cause a multitude of different emotions and they all come from your thoughts.

Using Thought Records

Thought records or diaries are often used in cognitive behavioral therapy as a way of getting a person to pay proper attention to their thoughts and to get them to work on ways to change them. While this might seem like an awful lot of work to start with, as time goes by, it becomes an automatic process and the diaries will soon not be needed.

CBT thought diaries are useful for the person making the entries as well as for the medical professionals. The person can read through the events they have written down, they can monitor their own thoughts and see where it is possible to make changes. To be of the absolute best use, these diaries should be use several times a week after any situation that provokes anxiety, even a small amount.

Unhelpful Thoughts

Most people who have social anxiety disorder tend to have two types of negative thoughts. First, they will overestimate the likelihood of something truly bad happening and second, they will overestimate how bad the situation will be if that terrible thing happens. It is because of this, because of the unhelpful thoughts, that reality is distorted. The thoughts are not rational in terms of how that person perceives themselves, of how they perceive others and how they perceive the world. Core belief lies at the heart of most of the unhelpful thoughts, some of those core beliefs being that "everyone has to like me" or " I can't ever make any mistakes". Using the thought diaries on a regular basis will help a person to identify patterns in their thoughts and will also point the way to the core belief that lie behind the negative thoughts.

How to use Thought Records

When you first begin to use thought records, you may find it difficult to see your way around creating a better style of thinking. Given time and regular use, the new, better thoughts will soon become believable to the extent that they are the first thoughts you have.

Although many therapists will provide a form for you to complete for each diary entry, you can do whatever feels right to you, so long as your thoughts are recorded. What you must record is the following information:

The activating event

Describe in detail the event or situation that caused a strong negative reaction or emotion, such as anxiety or panic. It could be a situation that happened, a thought you had, a recollection, anything that triggered the emotion. Only write down the facts of the event

The consequences of the event

Describe what the consequences of the activating event were. Forget about your thoughts at this stage; write down what your feelings were, your emotions. How intense, on a scale of 0 to 100, was the emotion or feeling? (0 being the lowest and 100 being the highest.) Pick the one emotion or feeling that you most associate with what happened and underline it. Write down what, if any behaviors or actions you did or took part in while the event was happening.

Your beliefs about the event
Describe what your beliefs are about the event. This could include perceptions, attitudes, thoughts and expectations. Write down what you were thinking about at the time, what thought went through your head. Dig a little bit deeper and think about what is behind those thoughts. Ask questions like, "what does that say about me?" or "and this is bad, because?". Keep digging until you can identify the one thought that is the most distressing. Underline it and rate it, from 0 to 100, on how much you believe it.

Your unhelpful thought styles
Describe any thought styles you had that were unhelpful, in terms of relationship to your beliefs. Examples of unhelpful thought styles include mental filtering, thinking only in black and white, jumping quickly to conclusions. Over generalizing the situation, turning it into a catastrophe, personalizing it, labeling, magnifying and minimizing.

Your one unhelpful thought
Go back to that one unhelpful thought that you underlined and evaluate it. The real key to being able to change your thought patterns lies in your ability to challenge the thoughts that you have. Consider the evidence that there is, both for and against that one thought, that one belief that stands out above all others. How realistic is that thought? If you didn't suffer from anxiety, how would the situation have played out? Is there anything that you are ignoring, any other explanation? Ask yourself how another person would see the situation and how he or she would react. Be very objective about the thoughts you have.

Replacing that thought
Finally, based on what you discovered in the last bit, write out some alternative thoughts, thoughts that are more balanced,

thoughts that can replace that unhelpful one and turn the situation around. Then, go back and find the emotion that you most closely associate with the event and rate it again, followed by rating how much belief you now have in the original unhelpful thought.

Chapter 13 – Let's Get Physical…And Calmer

One thing that's often taken for granted, especially when it comes to managing and coping with social anxiety – or any other anxiety disorder – is physical exercise. Studies have shown that apart from lowering your risks for heart disease, stroke, high blood pressure, diabetes and obesity, regular physical exercise can also be beneficial when it comes to managing social or any other forms of anxiety disorder. Exercising is one great way to naturally relieve anxiety and manage stress levels.

Exercise And Physical Activities: One And The Same?

Many people assume the two are one and the same. So if you assumed the same, don't feel bad and stress over it. You won't go to jail for assuming such. Apart from muscle contractions, the two are very much different.

When you say physical activity, you talk about any movement, which causes muscle contraction. Anything. You blink your eye, that's physical activity. When you take out the trash, that's physical activity. When you eat, that's physical activity.

Exercise is a form of physical activity but it differs from all others in terms of being specific. While physical activities differs in purpose – from keeping the house clean to grabbing a bite – exercise is done deliberately in terms of duration, intensity and movement with the goal of improving physical strength and stamina and cardio vascular health. Exercise activities include hoisting barbells and dumbbells in the gym, running for 5 kilometers at the oval track or swimming, among others.

Speaking of intensity, the term is defined as the amount of effort you exert in doing something. In exercise terms, it's measured in terms of Metabolic Equivalents or MET. This simply refers to the ratio of your exercising metabolic rate over your resting or base metabolic rate. One unit of MET consumes an estimated 1 calorie per kilo of body weight every hour.

There are different intensity levels when it comes to exercising but these are generally classified as light, moderate or vigorous or high intensity. There's a very technical – and geeky, by the way, method of estimating your current exercise intensity level but of course, who has time to waste for that? The simplest but relatively good way to estimate your current exercise intensity is through the talk test.

The talk test goes like this. While exercising, try to talk. If you can talk normally without any effort, you're exercising at low intensity. If you can still talk clearly but with some effort, then your exercise intensity is moderate. If you can hardly talk and are struggling to catch your breath, that's high intensity.

The Right Intensity For Anxiety Management

When it comes to managing and coping with your social anxiety, the optimal exercise intensity is moderate. Why? Low intensity is way too easy to make any meaningful impact such as weight loss, which can go a long way towards improving your self-esteem and consequently, reducing social anxiety.

High intensity is counterproductive, as it will make you even more stressed and can aggravate your anxiety symptoms.

Since your goal is to cope with and manage your social anxiety well, the last thing you need is more stress and anxiety symptoms right? Right!

Moderate exercises lasting at least 30 minutes done thrice a week is optimal. It's neither too easy to make any significant impact nor too stressful to aggravate your existing anxiety issues.

Chapter 14 – Social Anxiety In Children

Social anxiety disorders aren't just confined to adults – children can suffer from them too. Children who do suffer from social anxiety and phobia are primarily scared of being criticized. One way they normally express such anxiety is by asking things like:

- What if do or say a stupid thing?
- What if I speak or act wrongly?

Another way young children express social anxiety and phobia is by crying and throwing tantrums when they are faced with situations that scare them and these behaviors are often misinterpreted as merely being hard-headed, stubborn or worse, being spoiled brats. The fear that causes such behavior can result in the manifestation of social anxiety symptoms like shortness of breath, sweating and shaking. Worse, these can also interfere with their normal, daily activities as these may occur far in advance of the actual situation or event that can trigger it. The fear or dread children with social anxiety feel is greatly out of proportion to the actual thing they fear may happen or its consequences.

Performance And Interaction

When it comes to children's social anxiety, there are 2 main types: performance and interaction.

Children may experience social anxiety attacks as triggered by things like ordering food in restaurants, speaking in front of the class, buying candy from the store and even praying in front of a small group of people. These events or activities are related to doing things or "performing" and those who suffer from this type of social anxiety fear being judged, ridiculed or humiliated in case they screw things up, no matter how minor or trivial the mistake may be.

Children may also experience social anxiety episodes triggered by simply being around people – interacting with them. Trigger situations may include using a public restroom, going to the arcade, attending a birthday party, going to church, going to the doctor, going to the hospital and attending a family reunion, among others. It is often the case that children who suffer from interactional social anxiety also suffer from performance social anxiety.

How Do Children Get It?

One way children suffer from social anxiety is through genetics – it's hereditary. It's observed to be more common in children who have a parent or other 1st-degree relatives who have the disorder.

Another way that children may suffer from it is through experience. A child who may have suffered a traumatic social experience may experience social anxiety disorder. Take for example, children who are bullied in school. Since bullying is a social event and often happens in front of many other children, the humiliating experience may be impacted on the child's psyche and he or she may learn to associate it with being with other children. It may also be that the social anxiety is genetic but the manifestation was triggered by traumatic experience – a combination of the two.

Does Your Child Have Social Anxiety Disorder?

For your child to be diagnosed with social anxiety disorder, he or she must have a severe enough fear of being humiliated in social interactions to the point that daily normal functioning is already impaired. He or she will most likely do his or her best to stay away from situations or events that he or she feel are directly related to their anxiety for fear of suffering their potential consequences. Your child, if with social anxiety disorder, may experience a very acute form of anxiety and can manifest social anxiety symptoms such as profuse sweating, trembling and shortness of breath. Younger children may throw tantrums and cry as an expression of their social anxiety episodes. Another way a child's anxiety may be triggered is when he or she feels that he or she will be negatively judged or even punished for merely looking anxious.

For your child to be considered as having social anxiety disorder, the anxiety must manifest while in the presence of his or her peers instead of just being with adults and must have been persisting for more than 6 months already. The only person who can conclusively and validly diagnose your child for social anxiety disorder is a licensed medical professional.

It may be possible that your child, if he or she has it, may either deny feeling anxious in social situations or downplay the symptoms of such for fear of being judged, scrutinized or even embarrassed. When this happens, the diagnosing medical professional will have to speak with you (parents), nannies and teachers to get a better understanding of the symptoms he or she is manifesting and make an accurate evaluation and diagnosis of such.

Treatments

If your child is officially diagnosed with social anxiety disorder, don't lose hope. It's because social anxiety is a very treatable condition that responds very well to behavioral therapy, minimizing the need for prescription medicines at such a young age. The goal of therapy is simply to help your child change his or her way of thinking as the primary form of coping with or managing social anxiety. Even for children who are under a combined program of behavioral therapy and prescription medicines, behavioral therapy works well to the point that they don't take the medicines for long.

Behavioral Therapy

With behavioral therapy, a licensed therapist will most probably begin with cognitive behavioral therapy (CBT) to help improve your child's coping and social skills in situations that can trigger their social anxiety. CBT helps your child to learn that they actually have the power to manage or control their undesirable reactions and anxiety. Therapy teaches them to overcome fear and modify their anxious thinking patterns.

Another type of therapy – exposure therapy – involves gradually exposing them to situations that trigger their anxiety in a very controlled manner with the goal of getting them used to such situations and over time, reduce or minimize their anxiety episodes during such situations.

Prescription Medicines

In case behavioral therapy isn't enough, doctors may prescribe medicines for your child's social anxiety to help alleviate it. In many cases, prescription medicines help behavioral therapy more effective and as mentioned earlier, these are usually taken for a short period of time only.

As with adult social anxiety, your child's doctor may prescribe selective serotonin reuptake inhibitors (SSRI) or beta blockers. These medicines can help reduce your child's anxiety by curbing their fearful responses to situations that trigger social anxiety as well as minimizing the physical symptoms of such like profuse sweating, palpitations and shortness of breath.

Chapter 15 - 11 Things You Should Do if You Have Social Anxiety Disorder

While having a social anxiety disorder can be debilitating, there are plenty of things you can do to help yourself, like the following 11 suggestions:

1. Start Socializing

While it can be extremely tempting to stay away from social situations when you have an anxiety disorder, the most important thing you can do is to get out there and be seen. That means that, instead of turning them down, you should accept invitations and go to places that make you uncomfortable. At the same time, make sure you are mentally prepared to handle whatever you may face.

2. Get Some Help

Don't leave it, don't wait. If you haven't sought out any help, you need to do it now It's no god putting it off or waiting until you next fall into a crisis, make that appointment today. If you think that you will be embarrassed to speak to your own doctor about it, call a mental health helpline, just to take that first step. You might find that speaking to a faceless stranger on the phone is much easier and much less intimidating. It could be the one thing that leads to you getting the help that you need. Only you can take that first step though so do it today.

3. Develop Some Healthy Habits

Do all that you can to make sure that your physical health is up to scratch. Poor health can contribute to anxiety problems so make sure you get plenty of exercise, including some weight training and cardiovascular exercise, and take a long hard look at your diet. If you at mainly junk and unhealthy foods, make some serious changes today. Stay away from alcohol and caffeine and, if you feel anxious, drink chamomile tea.

4. Read

Read everything you can find about your anxiety disorder and what you can do to help improve it. Read stories about others who have overcome their anxiety and how they did it, what gave them the push to do it. Read plenty of motivational books on the subject of life. Education can't hurt you and it might just give you the push you need to start making changes to your own life and your own mental wellbeing.

5. Keep a Journal

Make sure you write in it daily so that you can monitor how well you have been improved. Write down your experiences and your thoughts because this will help you to recognize when you are dropping back to old habits and your unhelpful and negative thought patterns.

6. Congratulate Yourself

You may not be all that confident at public speaking but there are plenty of things in your life that you can be proud of. Recognize that, because of your anxiety disorder, you have to face more challenges than anyone does and, no matter how small they may be, you should feel proud of any accomplishment that you make in your life. Some days you might even be able to congratulate yourself just for making it out of the house. Build on the small achievements and you will start to feel so much better about yourself.

7. Write Your Goals Down

It simply isn't enough to be vague about the goals you want to achieve. It matters not what your goal is, whether it is to overcome all or a particular symptom of your social anxiety, or if you want to be become an award-winning author, it is vital that you write every goal down on paper. That way, they are real goals, they are measurable and you have something to look back on.

8. Become Your Own Advocate

The only person who can really look out for you is you and you are the best person for the job. So, gather up all the information you can about social anxiety disorder, or whatever type of anxiety disorder you suffer from. This will enable you to be able to make better decisions. Join self-help groups, talk to others and help people to understand the struggles that you face every single day. If you are at a social gathering and you really feel that you need to get away, take a bit of time out. Nobody but you knows what it is like to be you, to face what you do on a daily basis.

9. Practice Your Social Skills

Not everyone is born knowing how to be social, with the gift of the gab but you can always make some improvements on the skills that you do have. Practice making introductions; practice making better eye contact, practice remembering names and learn how to give out compliments. If you want to polish up your public speaking skills or just become more confident, look to see if there are any courses you can take at your local college or university.

10. Practice Assertiveness Skills

Two things that go together are social anxiety and a real lack of assertiveness. The real problem when you are not assertive is that other people are not given the chance to help you or to meet your needs. Understand the difference between assertiveness and aggressiveness – they are not the same thing. Being assertive is all about going after what you want but not in an aggressive manner – it is about being clear, right from the start, what you need.

11. Share Your Experiences

Whether you are half way through conquering your social anxiety or you have managed it, what you have been through is valuable so share it with other people. Join anxiety groups and talk to others, tell them of your struggles and how you overcame them. It will help others to realize that there is a light at the end of the tunnel and that they are not alone. It will also help to make people aware of a problem that is kept firmly locked away behind closed doors.

Chapter 16 - 10 Things You Need to Stop Doing if You Have Social Anxiety Disorder

Having a social anxiety disorder is nothing to be ashamed of. You are most definitely not alone but while there are lots of things you should be doing, there are also some things you have to stop doing.

1. **Stop Avoiding**

Avoidance comes in many guises. Some people drink a lot when they go to social gatherings, just to give them the courage they need to get through the night. Some people won't make eye contact when they talk to others or they may read a speech word for word. No matter what it is, no matter how subtle it is, you must stop the avoidance tactics; they only make things worse over the long term

2. **Stop the Negative Thoughts**

Negative thoughts are one of the root causes of social anxiety disorder. As we discussed earlier, there are several forms of treatment for anxiety disorder, such as Acceptance and Commitment Therapy (ACT) or cognitive-behavioral therapy (CBT) that have their basis in identifying and changing negative thought processes. If you are struggling on where to begin, start to keep your own thought diary – this will tell you how often you have negative thoughts and then you can begin to work on changing them.

3. **Don't Put Off Getting Help**

If you think that you have an anxiety disorder but have not yet been properly diagnosed, it is time to take the step of getting some help. It will probably be the most difficult step you ever have to take but it will be the start of a new way of life for you. Being properly diagnosed is the only way to get the right help so have a chat with your doctor. If your anxiety stops you from doing this, write it all down, make the appointment and hand over what you have written.

4. Stop Believing That There is No Hope

There is always hope. You may believe that medication won't work or it has too many risks. You might think that therapy is for losers but, really, when you think about it, what do you have to lose by trying? There are properly established treatments for each anxiety disorder and you owe it to yourself to get your life back on track by giving them a try.

5. Stop Comparing Yourself

You are you. You are not someone else and the only time you will ever feel good when you compare yourself to others is when you are doing better than they are. Get used to the fact that there is always going to be someone who has more confidence than you do, who more socially adept or who has more friends. Instead of wasting time and energy comparing yourself to others, work on self-improvements. The real measure of your success is how well you are doing compared to a month ago, six months or a year ago. Not how you compare yourself to all the others around you.

6. Stop Telling Yourself You Can't Change

You might feel like you were dealt a rough hand or you might think that you are just too old for help. No matter what your reasoning is, stop right now. There is always room for change and everyone can do it. You just have to identify the things that you can change and do it while accepting the things that you can't change. Social skills can be improved with practice and, with the right exposure, you can be more comfortable in social or performance situations.

7. Stop Predicting That You Will Fail

Because the more you do that, the more chance there is of you failing. Instead of thinking about the things you don't want happening, turn your attention to the things you do want to happen. If you are due to give a speech, think of yourself as confident and outgoing. If you have to attend a social gathering, imagine yourself as a real social butterfly. If these things don't happen, at least you can say you tried, that you gave yourself every chance.

8. Stop Missing Opportunities

Did you pass up on the offer of a promotion at work? Did you drop out of a college course or is it that you haven't stepped out of the house for a long time, despite the opportunity to do so? If this is you, you care allowing your social anxiety disorder to rule your life, to make you miss out on opportunities. You will end up with a lot of regrets about the things you didn't do or didn't try. If you make a mistake, at least you will know that you have tried, that you went for it. Do not let your anxiety disorder take you over and stop you from getting what it is you want from life.

9. Stop Keeping Your Disorder a Secret

Social anxiety disorders tend to foster an aura of shame. You fear that others will suddenly find out that you suffer from anxiety that you can't cope too well in social situations. Why hide it? Start being honest, with yourself and with others. There is no need to walk up to a stranger and tell that you suffer from social anxiety disorder, although hats off to you if you do because that means you have overcome a huge hurdle!

You can tell you nearest and dearest though, tell them what makes you anxious, Far from laughing and pointing at you, they will go out of their way to help you and, one day, you may even be comfortable enough to tell them everything.

10. Stop Believing That You Suffer Alone

One of the biggest problems with anxiety disorders is that you spend so little time talking to other people that you may not realize they have problems as well. You might think that everyone around you is confident when they are in a social situation but many of them are not. There are lots of people who suffer the same struggles that you do; talk to them, read other people's stories just so you know that you are not facing this alone.

Chapter 17 - 8 Things People with Social Anxiety Want

Just because you have a social anxiety disorder, it does not make you any different from anyone else. Like them, you want to connect with people, you want to achieve things and you want peace in your life. You also want a level of understanding from other people. If you suffer with an anxiety disorder, you might find that I am talking about you in one of these:

1. Connection

People who have social anxiety disorder may fear social situations, facing other people or interacting socially but they do still want people they can call friends. Very often, being on your own can cause feelings of depression and loneliness to set in. You can overcome your anxiety by getting the right treatment and by building up your social skills. You are not alone; we all feel a bit awkward when we try to make friends with someone new but it does get easier over time.

2. Understanding

More than anything else in the world, a person who has social anxiety disorder wants to be heard, they want to be understood, not just as a person but also in respect of their symptoms, of the struggles they face on a daily basis. Learning more about the disorder can help if you are trying to understand and help a friend or family member who has an anxiety disorder. If you suffer from the disorder and you are surrounded by people who do not understand, print an article that explains or leave a book that talks about it lying around.

3. Solitude

As much as a person with social anxiety wants to be able to connect with others, they also need to be alone at times.

Sometimes, social anxiety will overlap with introversion and this can be the perfect time to let your batteries recharge and your strength gather up for another go at interacting. Extroverts get their strength from being surrounded by other people but introverts sometimes need to be alone to make themselves feel better. If you are an introvert, don't apologize for needing time to yourself, even if you are in the middle of a social gathering.

4. Stability

Especially emotional stability, which is one of the biggest goals of many people with social anxiety disorder. Some want to be able to manage their feelings, thoughts and emotions better, to understand exactly what triggers off their symptoms of anxiety. They want to know how they can balance out their emotions when they face those situations. Sometimes it is better to just be at peace, at one with your feelings, rather than trying to control the anxiety.

5. Peace

When you suffer with social anxiety, there are quite a few ways that you can achieve peace. You can take up yoga, mindfulness meditation, deep breathing or any other practice that is designed to create an awareness of a situation and to bring your mind in tune with your body. ACT (Acceptance and Commitment Therapy) is one of the treatments on offer that can help you to take advantage of these kinds of exercises while you work on reducing the symptoms of your anxiety

6. Confidence

For some people with anxiety disorder, confidence is their biggest goal. Confidence can only grow when you are prepared to face down your fears and work to overcome them. Face the situations that bring fear to your life and build up your confidence slowly. Eventually, the triggers that started your symptoms will have less effect and you will have the confidence you need to cope.

7. Fulfillment

Some people who have social anxiety disorder feel that they cannot achieve their goals because of the disorder. This interferes with how fulfilled they feel with life. Everyone needs a purpose in life, everyone needs goals and being able to face the fears and achieve the goals can bring a real sense of fulfillment and achievement.

8. Growth

Many people who have social anxiety disorder want to experience personal growth. They will read any self-help books and look at other stories on how people have overcome their fears so that they can learn how to grow and better themselves.

Chapter 18 - 10 Anxiety Myths Busted

Are you one of those that has been telling yourself that you will get better, that you do not need any help? If you are it's time to look at these 10 myths about anxiety that I am going to bust right out of the water. Part of what may be stopping you from getting the help you need is that, in general, you may well be functioning ok. More often than not, a person with an anxiety disorder can seem like nothing more than a habitual worrier, rather than someone who may be struggling with a mental health disorder. Even so, you may not be living the life of fulfillment that you really want to live. The true extent of your anxiety disorder will have a strong influence on your decision of whether to seek treatment or not. Read the following well; it could be the thing that makes you take the first step.

Anxiety Disorders Are Not Real Illnesses

Everyone suffers from a certain amount of anxiety in his or her life, it's only natural. Sometimes it is even very helpful. However, an anxiety disorder is a very extreme form of the mild, occasional anxiety that we all feel and it can be extremely debilitating to the extent that it causes serious impairment of judgment.

If you have ever been diagnosed with a serious disease, such as cancer, you will have been through a number of diagnostic tests in order to reach that diagnosis. Although there are no actual tests, no blood tests or scans that a person can have to diagnose social anxiety disorder, there are plenty of other ways it can be determined. That doesn't make it an illness that is not real because, believe me, it is very real especially to those who have it

Panic Attacks Make You pass Out or Lose Control

Passing out happens when a person experiences a sudden drop in blood pressure. That does not happen during a panic attack. In fact, the complete opposite happens. When a person suffers a panic attack, they experience a raise in blood pressure and an increase in heart rate and that anyone means that it is not possible to pass out when you are having a panic attack.

These attacks are dreadful, not just to experience but to see as well. Fear of having a panic attack makes them far worse and that is another good reason to seek treatment for anxiety disorders. It may interest you to know that at least 20 to 25% of the population has had a panic attack at some time or another, However, only about 2 to 3% have actually gone on to develop a panic or anxiety disorder. This disorder is a very vicious cycle – worrying about having the attacks is actually more likely to make them happen and they will be worse. Some of the treatment involves learning to accept panic attacks and to ride the wave when they happen because nothing bad is going to happen. That in itself can lessen the severity and the occurrences of the attacks.

People With Anxiety Should Avoid Stressful Situations

First of all, it is completely impossible to avoid situations that may be stressful. Second, if a person with anxiety disorder were to do that, they would be seeing themselves as fragile people and that can lead to the disorder symptoms being much worse. Avoiding stress is not always the best way to avoid anxiety although it may seem that it is. It isn't easy to avoid these situations and it is most definitely not effective. For a start, life is full of little stresses, situations that are unexpected and not all of them will trigger the symptoms in a person with anxiety disorder. If you get into the habit of avoiding situations and places that are likely to cause anxiety, all you are doing is reinforcing the disorder, Effective treatment will involve the safe and gradual exposure to the source, the triggers of your anxiety symptoms, teaching you how to cope, not avoid it

You Should Always Have a Paper Bag In Case Of Hyperventilation

It is not true that hyperventilation is always dangerous and having to carry a paper bag with you all the time does nothing more than heighten the anxiety. It is considered to be a safety behavior, something that is based purely on the fear that something bad will happen and that you must have a plan to cope with it. Yes, you do need to have a plan but not a paper bag. Safety behaviors are nothing more than avoidance techniques, and they stop you from reaching down to the cause of the anxiety disorder.

Some People are Habitual Worriers and Can't Be Treated

There is most likely a genetic part to anxiety but the right treatment can help to get it under control, be it therapy or medication. A recent review determined that around two-thirds of the anxiety disorders diagnosed are most likely inherited. You do not need to accept that you are a habitual worrier and put up with it for life because the disorder can be treated successfully. The most effective treatment is CBT – cognitive behavioral therapy – in a recent study of 134 adults being treated for anxiety disorders, it was found that cognitive behavioral therapy educed the symptoms much more effectively within 3 months than any of the other more typical approaches did. The study also found that the positive effects of the therapy lasted for at least a year; CBT is all about identifying thoughts and behaviors that are positive and finding alternatives for the negatives.

Anxiety Disorders are Uncommon

In fact, they are not. Around 18% of the US population, almost one in five people, has some kind of anxiety disorder in any year that you care to examine. Although millions of people live with an anxiety disorder, many are very surprised to learn that they do not suffer alone. However, it is easy to understand why they might think that they are the only one because some anxiety disorders, particularly social anxiety disorder and obsessive compulsive disorder, can truly leave people isolated. You may never meet another person with an anxiety disorder until you take the step of reaching out for help. A recent study showed that the most common types of anxiety disorder are:

- A specific phobia – 12.1% of adults
- A social phobia – 7.4% of adults
- Generalized anxiety disorder – 2% of adults
- Separation anxiety disorder – 1.2% of adults
- Panic disorder – 2.4% of adults
- Obsessive compulsive disorder – 1.2% of adults

Anxiety Will Get Better On Its Own

No, it really will not. On average, a person with an anxiety disorder may wait around 10 years before they seek treatment for it. Those who can still go to work and function as "normal" tend to wait longer, hoping that it will just get better and go away by itself. The reality is, it doesn't. The reality is, you are most likely making things worse by waiting. On top of that, around 60% of those who have an anxiety disorder also have depression and that requires separate treatment.

I Just Need a Drink or a Smoke to Get Through It

One of the most common forms of treatment seen amongst people with anxiety disorders is self-medication. However, this is not effective and can very easily make things much worse. For some people, a drink or two may help them to get through an event without too much anxiety but self-medicating, be it with alcohol, drug, even cigarettes, is just another way of avoiding the truth, of avoiding the disorder rather than seeking treatment for it. Self-medicating can also be detrimental in the long run. Research shows that people who have an anxiety disorder are up to two times more likely to smoke than someone who does not. Not only does smoking, drinking or taking drugs not tackle the underlying cause of the anxiety, it also affects your health. It increases the risk factors of heart disease, lung disease, liver disease, stroke and cancers significantly. Instead of falling into this trap, seek help for the anxiety and for addiction if you find that you cannot give up the substance that you chose to help you through it.

Therapy Will Take Up the Rest of My Life

Wrong. Improvement can be seen within a few sessions of cognitive behavioral therapy and that can be anything form a few days to a few weeks. Even those who seek treatment for their anxiety are under the mistaken belief that it will take forever for them to get better. Cognitive behavioral therapy provides you with the tools that you need to use every day and at least 755 of those who go down the route of CBT report a reduction in symptoms of at least 50%.

You Can Snap out of Anxiety

You cannot overcome an anxiety disorder without appropriate help and you certainly cannot just "snap out of it". If you do not have an anxiety disorder, you might think that someone who fears meeting new people, who fears social settings, being in an enclosed space, even fearing germs, is just being ridiculous. It is not uncommon for some people to say to those with an anxiety disorder that they should just "get over it". There is no magic cure, no wand that can be waved and all your anxiety just melts away. The people who say these things do not understand the depth of fear that a person has, the degree to which their anxiety disorder is affecting them

Anxiety is a very vicious cycle. Worry and fear lead to a person avoiding the disorder, avoiding the subject altogether and this leads only to a strengthening of that worry and fear. Breaking out of that cycle invariably requires the help of professionals so, rather than trying to fight it silently, alone, take the step of seeking that help. Of taking back the control over your life.

Chapter 19 - Frequently Asked Questions about Anxiety Disorders

Finally, to recap, these are the most commonly asked questions about anxiety disorders.

What are the most common anxiety disorders?

- Generalized anxiety disorder
- Obsessive compulsive disorder
- Panic disorder
- Post traumatic stress disorder
- Social anxiety disorder

What is generalized anxiety disorder?

Generalized anxiety disorder, or GAD as it is otherwise known, is a tension and anxiety that is exaggerated and will last for months on end. Around 6.8 million Americans are affected by it, equating to just over 3% of the population. People who have GAD anticipate catastrophic happenings and excessively worry about a lot of different things – money, health, work, car repairs, even appointments. GAD affects more women than men and the anxiety can reach a severe level that affects life and relationships.

Symptoms include headache, fatigue, tension and aches in the muscles, trembling, twitching, sweating, irritability, hot flashes and a difficulty swallowing. It usually starts gradually and can start at any time in life.

What is obsessive compulsive disorder?

Better known as OCD, this is an anxiety disorder in which a person exhibits ritualistic behavior caused by fearful ideas.

The obsessions are impulses or thoughts that are repetitive, perhaps through a fear of hurting someone or from falling ill through another person's germs. These can create anxiety and stress but, although the person does not want these feelings, they are quite unable to stop them from happening. Some of the behaviors that may be exhibited are frequent hand washing, frequent cleaning, constantly having to check that a light or electrical appliance is off.

What is panic disorder?

Panic disorder is when a person is gripped with repeated and unexpected intense fear that is normally accompanied by physical symptoms. Those include pains in the chest, palpitations, dizziness, shortness of breath or distress in the abdomen. Characteristics include a sudden paralyzing attack of terror or fear, coupled with excessive sweating, a pounding heart, feelings of faintness or dizziness and weakness. The person experiencing the attack may feel chilled or they may feel flushed. Their hands may be numb or they may have tingles in them and they may feel sick or feel as though they are being smothered. A panic attack usually produces the sensation of total unreality, a real fear of doom or the fear of losing control. Panic attacks can occur when a person is awake or asleep.

What is post traumatic stress disorder?

Otherwise known as PTSD, this usually occurs when a person has been subjected to a terrifying ordeal or event during which physical harm was threatened or actually suffered. The most common events are death, war, earthquake, car accident, fire or flood and it is common for people exposed to these situations to feel fear, sadness, worry or anger after these events. However, if the symptoms carry on, become very severe or the person finds themselves reliving the event, these are all signs of PTSD and the person may find it difficult to function properly.

What is social anxiety disorder?

This is an anxiety disorder that is characterized by excessive feelings of self consciousness and anxiety in social situations. It can be just one type of social situation or it can encompass all social situations. Some people fear speaking in public, others experience a real fear of just being around any person, be they a friend, family or a stranger.

What is stress?

Stress is a normal response to a situation in which a person feels threatened, upset or angry. It is a physical response, often known as the "fight or flight" syndrome and this is when the body responds to a certain situation by producing high levels of hormones, including adrenaline and cortisol. It is these hormones that get the body ready for action.

What are the main symptoms of stress in adults?

- **Cognitive** - Memory problems, an inability to concentrate properly, the likelihood of making poor judgments, anxious thoughts, racing thoughts, excessive worrying

- **Emotional** - Irritability, mood swings, short tempers, not being able to relax, feeling overwhelmed, agitated and lonely

- **Physical** - diarrhea, constipation, dizziness, nausea, pains in the chest, racing heartbeat

- **Behavioral** - eating more or eating less, sleeping too much or not being able to sleep, isolation, neglect of responsibilities, procrastinations, turning to alcohol, drugs or cigarettes to cope, nervous habits, like pacing or biting the nails

Are there any coping strategies that can help?

Yes, there are and the following are ten of the most common strategies used in dealing with stress or stressful situations:

- Keeping a realistic outlook
- Facing the fear
- Relying on the inner compass
- Turning to religion or spiritual practices
- Seeking social support and accepting it
- Imitating sturdier role models
- Staying in good physical shape
- Maintaining a mental sharpness
- Finding ways to accept that some things can't be changed
- Looking for meanings and opportunities in the face of adversity

Conclusion

I hope that you have found this eBook helpful. I have tried to give an understanding of what social anxiety is and what a person who has it may be feeling as well some techniques on how to face it down. Please remember, these techniques are not just a one off; they are things you can do for as long as you need to, for as long as you are gaining a benefit from them.

Social anxiety, indeed any anxiety disorder, can be extremely debilitating to the person who is suffering from it. I have tried to give you some coping suggestions as well as tell you about the medical and alternative therapies and treatments that are available. The only person who can determine if you need treatment or not is you but bear in mind that leaving it and hoping that your anxiety will just magically disappear by itself will just make things worse.

Anxiety does not go away on its own, we cannot wave a wand and make it all disappear but, on the other hand, if you seek the right kind of help early enough, the treatment or therapy does not need to last forever. In many cases, just a few sessions can give you enough help and the tools necessary for you to go out there and start your won course of treatment, your own healing process and to give you some strong coping mechanisms so that you can start living your life again, instead of letting the anxiety and the fear control you.

If you find that nothing has changed, that you still feel unable to face social situations without feeling socially anxious, it may be time to seek advice from your doctor. He or she can recommend other options that may be of more benefit to you.

The only way to deal with fear be it of a social situation, or any other fear that causes you severe anxiety, is to face it head on. Hiding away or avoiding triggers will just make the situation worse and you will be less likely to be able to cope when you are thrown into a situation that can trigger of an anxiety attack. Face your fears, stare them in the eyes and don't back down. Force your fears to retreat instead, force your fears to hand you back your life.

Think strong and you will be strong. Think positive and you will be positive. Banish negativity from your life for good and never let it darken your door gain, at least not to the extent where your life is taken over. And remember, telling people about your fears makes you a stronger person, not a weaker one, because it means that you are facing them.

Thank you for purchasing this book. If you found this book helpful, please be so kind as to leave a review to help me provide you with more beneficial books and resources!

Bonus

Social anxiety is just one aspect of your health and wellbeing, and I am certainly glad you started there. If you are interested is taking your health (and life ultimately!) to the next level, I recommend the guide below to learn other easy-to-follow techniques you can apply today!

P.S. If you think your health is unrelated to anxiety, then I encourage you to educate yourself on the gut microbiome and how healthy gut bacteria can help us feel relaxed and at ease. This report will help show you how!

<u>**FREE BONUS:** 23 Health Tips & Hacks You Probably Aren't Doing But Should Be to Reduce Fatigue, Improve Sleep and Recovery, Boost Sex Drive, and Heal Your Gut</u>

P.S. Check out my other books too if you found this one helpful.

Recommended Reading

Achieve Your Next Level Health With a Click Away:

Low Carb: Ketogenic Diet to Overcome Belly Fat, Lose Pounds, and Live Healthy

Health and Fitness: Uncommon HIGH Impact Quick Wins You Should Start Today - Nutrition, Natural Health, and Healthy Living

Intermittent Fasting: Shortcut to Build Muscle, Lose Fat, and Easy Weight Loss

Detox: Cleanse for Fast Weight Loss, Anti Aging, Holistic Healing and Better Health

Vegan: Vegan Diet for Easy Weight Loss and Healthy Living Through Natural Foods

Other Recommended Books to Become More Effective and Fulfilled In Life:

Self Improvement: Self Discipline - An Uncommon Guide to Instant Self Control, Incredible Willpower, and Insane Productivity

Spirit Guides: Ultimate Guide to Exploring the Spirit World, Finding Your Angel Guide and Mastering Spirit Communication

$10.77
4/13/16

51144877R00083

Made in the USA
Lexington, KY
13 April 2016